Shrunken Heads

A Workshop with Russ Adams

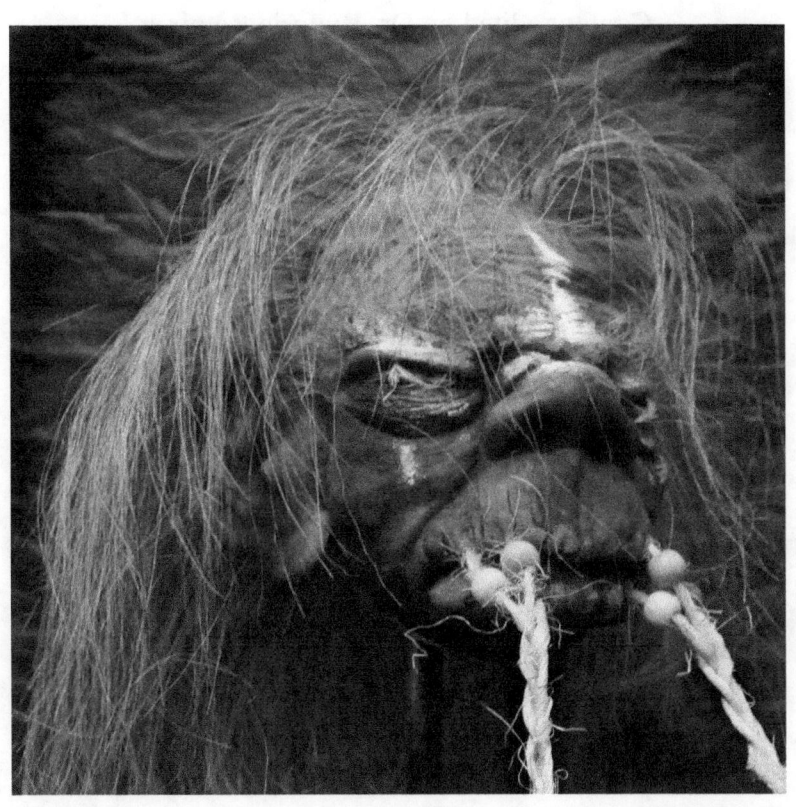

Photographs, layout, design, and Illustrations: Russ Adams
Text edited by Jan Hamer
Content edited by Dr. Victoria Ramirez

Published in the United States of America by
Old Scottish Bastard Media, LLC
1501 W 2650 S STE 105
Ogden UT, 84401

ISBN-13: 978-1542948265

ISBN-10: 1542948266

Russ Adams's websites
Author Page: www.russadams.me
Professional Page: www.escapedesignfx.com

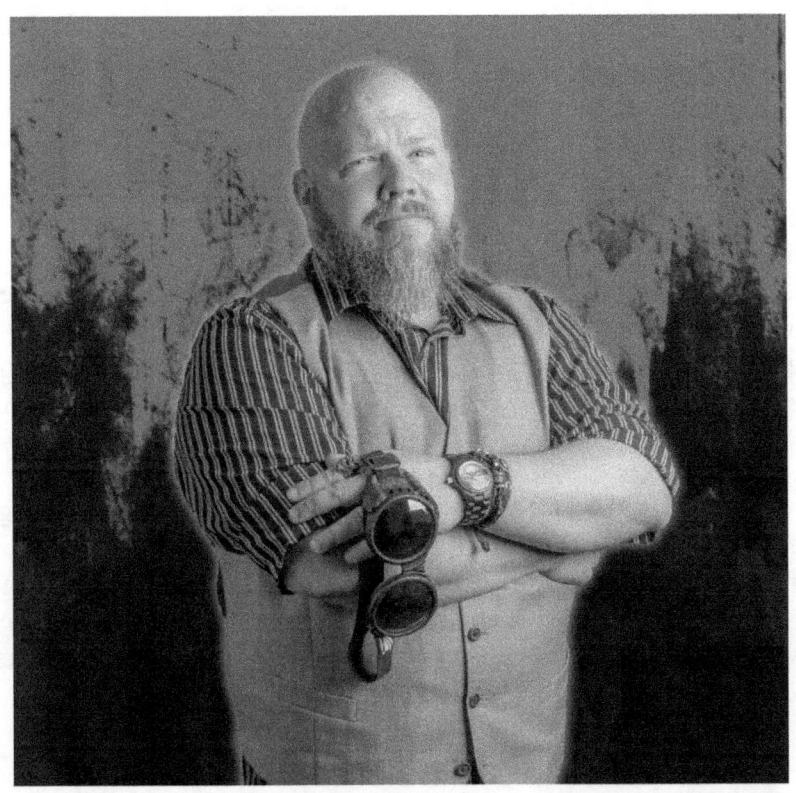

About the Author

I am well-known special-effects artist. I own a studio called Escape Design FX in Utah. I have also worked in the industry for nearly 20 years. My work has been seen in countless films, on television, and commercials. Because of my time on the highly-rated skill-based reality series, *Jim Henson's Creature Shop Challenge*, I travel the world teaching puppet creation, makeup effects, and mask making. As you probably noticed, I am also an author with a series of how-to books.

Not too shabby for a farm kid from rural Pennsylvania.

Author Site: (http://www.russadams.me)
Escape Design FX: (http://www.escapedesignfx.com)

People praise my masks, creature suits, and yep, even my shrunken heads. They liken my work to wearable works of art, which I greatly appreciate. I try to build things that look just as good on display as they do on a person's body. My masks range from simple eye covers to enormous Torso Masks ™ and creature suits. What I love most about doing what I do is having the opportunity to drag a concept into the real world and sharing it with everyone.

My family didn't have a ton of money, so if I wanted something the most likely way of getting it was to build it myself. It's not surprising that I would eventually work in a field where making things from nothing is the name of the game. I started selling my own line of masks after I founded Escape Design FX. And it has been a blast ever since.

 For you, it all starts here. Now, I'd like to share what I've learned with you.

In this book, you will find detailed, step-by-step instructions on how to create your very own latex masks. I've included a list of all the materials you'll need at the beginning of each section. I have also added a checklist at the end of the book as a quick reference guide when you start molding your sculpture. Between the contents of the book, and that checklist, you have all the tools to produce a killer shrunken head and mold to make as many copies as you like.

Let's get started!

Books by the Same Author

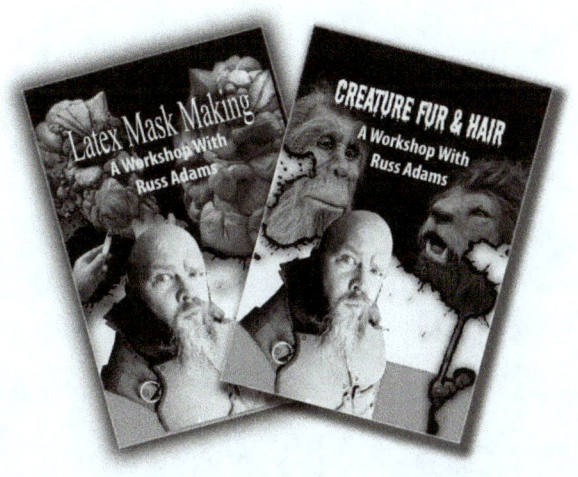

Table of Contents

PREFACE

My goal for this book is to give you the tools to succeed in your shrunken-head-making endeavor by guiding you through a step-by-step process that will increase your odds of success. In this book, you are going to learn more than just how to make shrunken heads: in addition to teaching you the process, I am going to rescue you from the idea that you need to buy specialized tools and equipment to succeed in any of your future projects.

My philosophy is, "Don't buy it, build it." By creating your own tools, you save money—money that could go toward more clay, plaster, or education. A sculpting tool with some other artist's name or studio printed on it isn't going to help you sculpt any better. These tools are likely poorly made imports marked up to line the pockets of the greedy. So, "Don't buy it, build it." If you must buy it, look at all the options. We will talk more about this in the section called STEP 2: Making Your Sculpting Tools.

In this tutorial, I am going to show you how to use found items and put them to work for you. I am also going to show you how to recapture and revitalize some materials to make them last longer.

When we are done, I hope to have taught you a few things, but I also hope to instill a greater appreciation for the cost and craftsmanship that go into handmade items created by other artists. When you go to a trade show, artists markets, or indie artist's website and see their handcrafted work on display, you will have an appreciation for the work because you will have experienced it firsthand.

Finally, when you order *A Workshop with Russ Adams* you will receive the full lesson from start to finish. For that reason, you may encounter a few steps that also appear in my other books. This is because I wrote each of these books as stand-alone or self-contained workshop—unlike most special effects tutorials that drag a project out across two or three books or videos.

In this book, *Shrunken Heads: A Workshop with Russ Adams*, I discuss the entire process, which includes sculpting, molding, casting, seaming, cleaning, painting, and hair punching, as well as the tool-making instructions mentioned above. I will not pause in the middle of the process and continue the workshop in another book. While I would like you to order other workshops, I would prefer you did so because you trusted me and wanted to learn a new special-effects process.

A NOTE ON SAFETY

WARNING

You will be using chemicals to create your shrunken head, so please make sure you read the safety instructions that come with those materials, and take all necessary precautions to ensure a safe working environment. I will do my best to remind you, but it's your responsibility to keep yourself and your working environment safe.

While latex really is a fun material to work with, some people are allergic to it. Basically, the symptoms run the gamut from mild: hives, itching skin, maybe a stuffy or runny nose, to breathing issues, and even chest-tightening and blood-pressure issues. Stronger reactions can also occur, including asthma-like symptoms or even anaphylactic shock. So please be careful. If you don't know whether you are allergic to latex, don't just dive in. Consult a doctor on the best way test for this if you suspect it.

Finally, a word about plaster. It seems harmless enough, but when plaster is setting, it can heat up to as much as 140 degrees Fahrenheit. It's unlikely to occur but be careful, you can easily burn yourself.

Breathing plaster dust is no fun for your lungs either, and of course just working with the stuff over time can dry out your skin. Make sure you clean it off thoroughly after each work session, wear gloves, a dust mask or respirator, and use lotion to keep your skin hydrated.

Basically, please be smart about your tools and materials. Do that and everything should be fine.

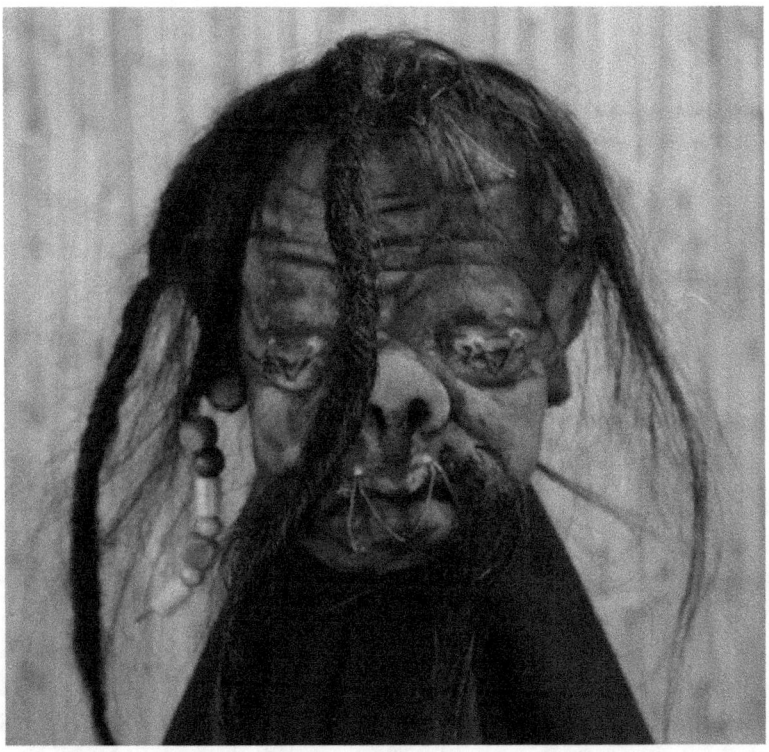

INTRODUCTION

I truly enjoy making shrunken heads. I am known for them. In fact, even before I became a special-effects artist I was fascinated by them. They are gruesome, but more than that the idea of them and what a shrunken head represents appeals to the dark-arts geek within. While much of what we have seen of shrunken heads are gaffs, or in other words, fakes, the process was very real and there are still real heads rolling around out there.

The materials used to create artificial, or gaff, shrunken heads are generally easy to find and they are relatively affordable compared to some of the materials we special-effects and prop artists use.

As of the time of this publication, I could pick up a gallon of latex for about forty-five dollars. That amount, if used properly, could yield up to a couple dozen shrunken heads—maybe more depending on size and surface space.

Plaster, UtlraCal 30, is also generally easy to find as well. You can purchase it online from mask and art supply houses or from a local foundry supply. The price is around thirty-five to forty dollars for fifty pounds. If you can find a local foundry supply, you can get a hundred pounds at roughly the same price as the fifty pounds you would buy at an art supply store. So, it pays to look around. A one-hundred-pound bag can yield as many as ten shrunken head molds depending on the size of the molds and your experience level.

The clay is another inexpensive material. The standard is WED clay (aka EM-217). It was developed long ago for Disney. In fact, WED is an acronym for Walt E. Disney. This is a water-based clay with a glycerin additive. It's an amazing material designed to produce large sculptures very quickly. You can find the clay at most ceramics stores, special-effects supply houses, or online. WED generally runs about twenty to twenty-five dollars for a fifty-pound box. Keep that in mind if you order online. Shipping is going to be quite a bit for a box that heavy. Then there is the treatment that package is going to receive by delivery personnel. I am sure you have seen the YouTube videos of delivery service personnel throwing, kicking, dropping, and generally mistreating packages. At any rate, a fifty-pound box of WED Clay goes a long way.

Once you get the process of making these little guys down, your imagination is the limit to what you can come up with next and how you can use them. I have seen my shrunken heads adorning the rearview mirror of many automobiles. They have graced countless book shelves, desks and have even been used as ornaments on a macabre Christmas tree. Gross! But I love it.

Shrunken Heads

I also use them to punch up characters. A good example would be the Skeksi I built on the highly rated Syfy skill-based reality television series, *Jim Henson's Creature Shop Challenge*. My teammates (Ivonne Escoto and Tina Roland) and I participated in a Dark Crystal challenge in episode two of the show. The challenge set forth was to create a Skeksi that had been banished to a distant land. My team drew an arid desert as our setting.

If you haven't seen the 1980s Henson classic *The Dark Crystal*, the Skeksis were the reptilian-avian antagonist race. It was a great movie and a huge source of inspiration for many up-and-coming special-effects artists.

I hung several shrunken heads from the shell Ivonne built. To me, these heads spoke volumes about the Skeksi's character. At a glance, they told a horrific backstory about this ghoulish critter. When it came time for our screen test, the judges asked us to discuss our banished Skeksi. I told the judges that our Skeksi was so sinister that he had taken slaves during his exile and worked them to death. Angered by their frailty, he shrank the corpses' heads, sending a message to the other slaves. They would continue to serve him even in death, if only to adorn his robes. Now that is dark—even for a Skeski.

If you are asking yourself, "What can I do with a shrunken head?" I would reply, "What CAN'T you do with a shrunken head! And why would you even ask that?"

COMMON FEARS

The biggest fear most people face coming into a project like this is the unknown. *Where do I begin? Will I be good at sculpting? Material costs are so expensive; can I even afford them? What if I screw something up?* These are all legitimate concerns and I am going to help you through them.

Where to start is probably the biggest problem most people have. It was for me. I grew up in the 1980s, the golden age of practical effects. There are all kinds of idols out there, and when you are a kid they vacillate between superheroes, actors, and musicians. Mine were special-effects artists--Rick Baker, Steve Johnson, Stan Winston, and Dick Smith. These were just a few of the men I looked up to as kid from rural Pennsylvania with delusions of working in the film business.

As a kid, I really wanted to know how they made all those wonderfully disgusting critters. Back then, the "how-to" of practical effects was about as well guarded as Fort Knox— perhaps unintentionally so. There were no YouTube tutorials cracking the code on makeup processes. There was no Amazon or Google search to find a how-to book on creature building. If you were interested and wanted to know more, you were stuck sifting through geriatric card catalogues and microfiche slides. Gods! I feel old right now.

My school library was a joke. I graduated with like sixty other teens. That should give you reference as to how vast my school library was. I am sure you can image the size and scope of the library's Hollywood practical-effects section. I had a consuming hunger to learn and the only thing at my disposal was grainy photos in magazines like Fangoria with the occasional shot of a creature in progress.

I learned by studying those photos like a thief casing a bank. Slowly, over the course of several years and tens of thousands of dollars, I started to figure things out.

You have the benefit of learning in an open-source world. YouTube is full of information to help you get started. There are classes and how-to books to help and easy-to-access search engines to find them. And you have me: a self-taught special-effects artist who learned the hard way and understands that you don't have a ton of money, and that you are worried about doing it right.

Some of you might be concerned about your ability, but don't be. I am going to teach you the steps we professional artists use to sculpt. I am going to slow you down to a comfortable pace and teach you to think about things in a different way. This is going to help you with your first creation and carry through to those that follow. This information will make you a more successful artist.

I am also going to teach you how to make your own tools to save you a fortune. You'll learn to make your own armatures, sculpting tools, turntables, and finishing tools. You may choose to purchase these things. That's fine. But you will be given the option to do it yourself and become self-sufficient.

I will be here to help you avoid common beginner mistakes, which will minimize your stress over screwing something up. So, relax. Enjoy the ride.

HISTORY OF SHRINKING HEADS

Before we move to the first step of the sculpting process, I thought it would be a good time to share the dark history of shrinking heads. If your sculpting skills are lacking, don't be concerned. This may work in your favor with this project. Once you hear how this process was carried out, you will see why.

The practice of head shrinking isn't as outdated as you might think. I recently watched a *National Geographic* documentary called *Search for the Amazon Headshrinkers*. The film's crew traveled to South America to either debunk or substantiate a 1961 film of the process. Using clues from the film, the documentary's team found the village captured on film so many years before. They had come face to face with the people involved with ritualistic head shrinking...for real! Oddly enough, they came extremely close to finding the very man demonstrating the act in the film.

When the crew arrived in the village alleged to be the source of the footage, they shared the movie with the inhabitants, hoping to uncover the truth of the process. Not only did the villagers recognize the act, but one villager recognized the man performing the process in the film: it was his brother. The recording was authentic.

Head shrinking is an actual ritual performed by only a few South American tribes in Ecuador and Peru: the Aguaruna, the Archuar, the Huambisa, and the Shuar. This skilled practice was implemented as a means of punishment for severe crimes. But crime wasn't the only way a person could end up with a tiny head.

Warring tribes would take the heads of their enemies as trophies. The victor may have had a nifty prize to show the neighbors, but there was the small matter of the victim's ghost. Surely the fallen soldier would seek revenge. As the vanquisher, you certainly didn't want an angry ghost trying to get revenge. Who needs that headache?

I suppose the headhunter figured that the ghost was already angry, so let's just poke it with a stick. Let's keep the spirit of the victim from crossing over to the spirit world by pulling the skin off the skull and shrinking it down. And while we are at it, let's sew his eyes and mouth shut so he won't see us poking him with the stick and can't yell at us for doing it.

I joke, but I am not that far off the truth of it. These people are very superstitious. They would sew the eyes shut to keep the victim's spirit from getting revenge. You can't find what you can't see. The same principles apply to the mouth. The lips were sewn shut to prevent the victim from speaking evil against the individuals performing the ritual. Gruesome, right?

The process, on the other hand, was elegant. When these tribes shrank a human head, they carefully peeled the skin off the victim's skull. Damaging the skin or removing it in such a way as to tear flesh or pull out hair would be very bad for the practitioner. Once removed, they boiled the skin, then packed the…well, face sack…with straw and hung it out to dry over the smoke of a fire.

The nose and lips often appear larger on a shrunk head because of the mass of material inside the skin. When we are sculpting, I will remind you to embellish these areas.

Why is this important to know—other than to gross you out? The actual practice of shrinking heads misshapen the features of the face. These features are important for realism. Knowing the "how" helps you to sculpt and later paint a more accurate gaff. Since the process brutally warps the victim's facial features, a lack of sculpting skill might just play to the strength of these necessary attributes.

Shrunken Heads

These are also things to keep in mind for the finishing process. Think of all that soot from the smoke. Think of how that might change the skin color. Think of the fluids escaping from the skin as it shrinks. They would run out of the face and boil off in the heat, staining streaks on the surface of this poor guy's skin.

Now that you know how the real thing was done, let's get to creating your shrunken head. The sooner you finish, the sooner you can start poking it with a stick.

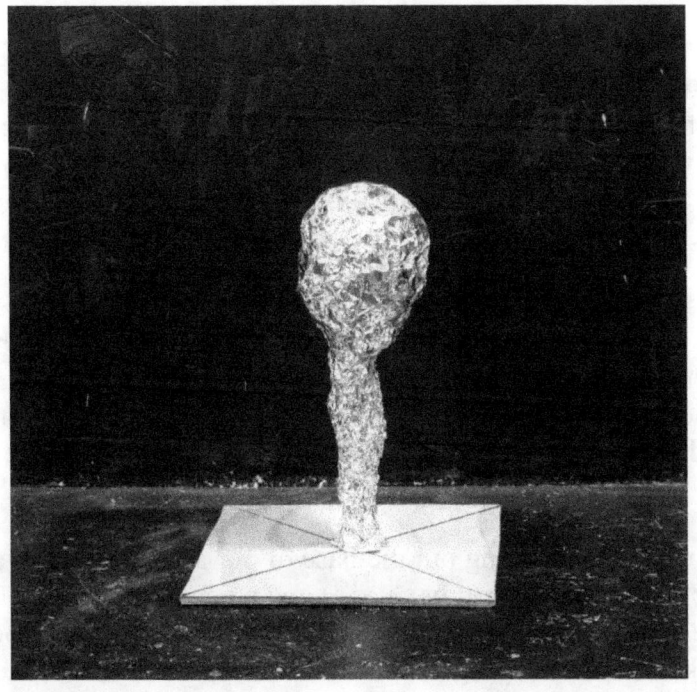

STEP 1: ARMATURES

Materials

1. 3/8" wood dowel 8 inches long
2. Scrap plywood (to cut a 6"x6" square from)
3. Glue (wood glue, Elmer's glue, hot glue)
4. Aluminum foil

Tools

1. Saw (scroll saw, jigsaw, hacksaw)
2. Straight edge (ruler, T-square, etc.)
3. Drill
4. 3/8" drill bit
5. Marker (or pencil)

Armature are critical in sculpting. They can offer stability, support, and give structure to your sculpture. And in some cases, they even save you from using large quantities of clay. There is a huge range of benefits to using an armature, but for this project it will serve as a support and allow you to use less clay.

Let's start with the wooden dowel. We are going to need the dowel to be about eight inches long. We are going to lose about a quarter of an inch or better when we insert the dowel into the plywood, depending on the thickness of the plywood. So, there should be about seven and half inches of material above the base plate.

Next, we will be cutting out the base of our armature. Take a ruler or T-Square (if you have one) and a pencil, then draw a square six inches by six inches. I suggest using scrap plywood. It always seems to be lying around and this makes use of something that would end up in the trash. Reduce, reuse, as much as you can.

The best way to cut this, in my opinion, is on a scroll saw. You can use a jigsaw, or even a hacksaw if that is what you have. The key is to be steady, slow, and safe.

Once the cuts are made we are going to find the center point of this square. We will use a pencil or a marker and a straight edge to trace a line across the square from one corner to the other. Repeat this on both sides of the plywood. When that's done, you will have an "X" on your square. The center of that "X" will give you the center of the square.

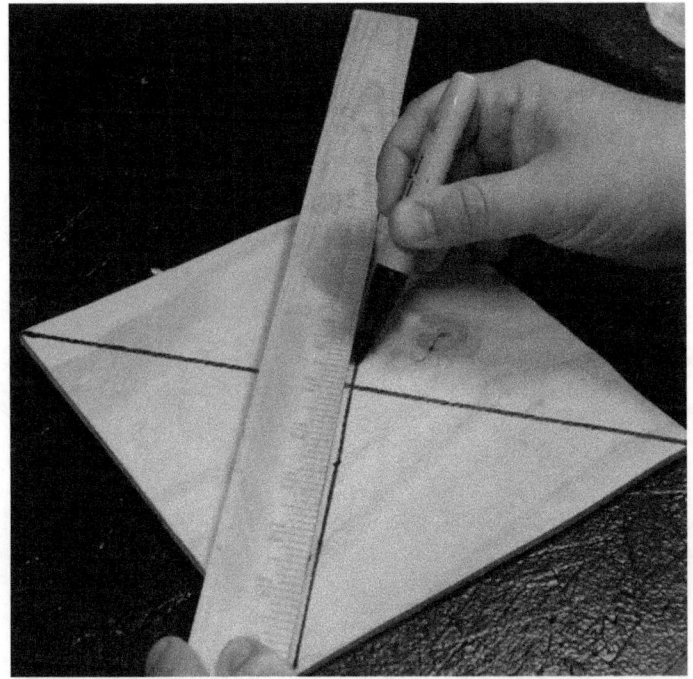

DIAGRAM 1

I have suggested that you use a three-eighths wooden dowel for this project. This will mean you will need a three-eighths drill bit for the project. If you only have a half inch wood dowel, then please make sure you have a matching drill bit.

Using a drill and a three-eighths inch drill bit, drill a hole into the center of that "X." This is where you will put your wooden dowel. Don't forget to put a drop of glue in the hole you drilled before you insert the dowel into it. You can use wood glue, Elmer's glue, or hot glue for this.

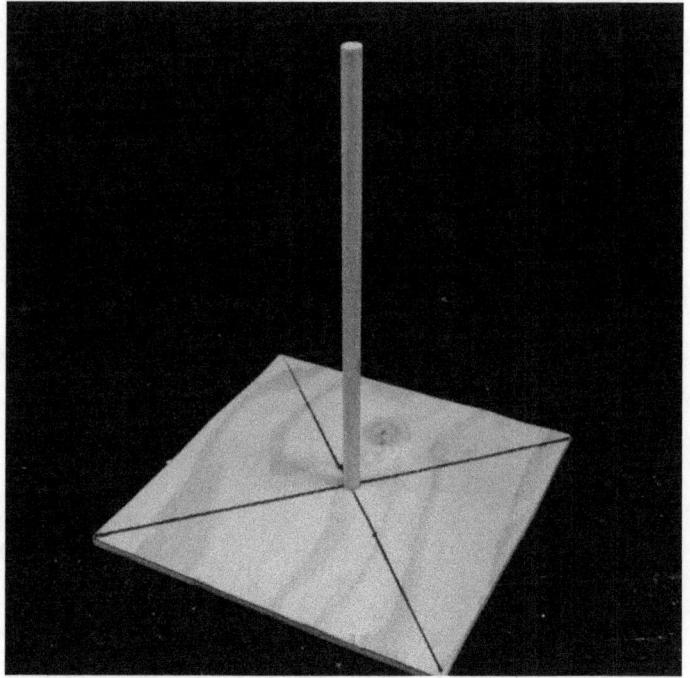

DIAGRAM 2

This is a basic armature and it cost you almost nothing.

If you are like me, and you try to conserve materials—especially clay—you can use aluminum foil to build a small mass, which you can sculpt over. This leaves you more clay to create your project and less used to build up a mass to get the size of the head you want.

I add glue to the surface of the dowel so that it holds the foil in place. I ball up a large amount of foil for the head, but I also use foil to build up the neck. The foil around the neck will help to keep the head in place. Plus, we will be building a neck at some point during the process, so we should be prepared.

Shrunken Heads

Congrats! This was our first project together in the workshop and you rocked it. You did rock it…right?

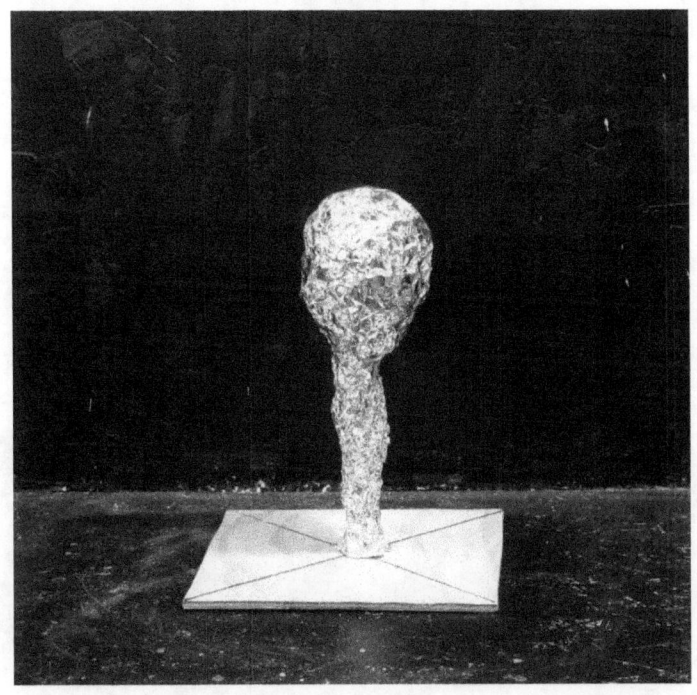

DIAGRAM 3

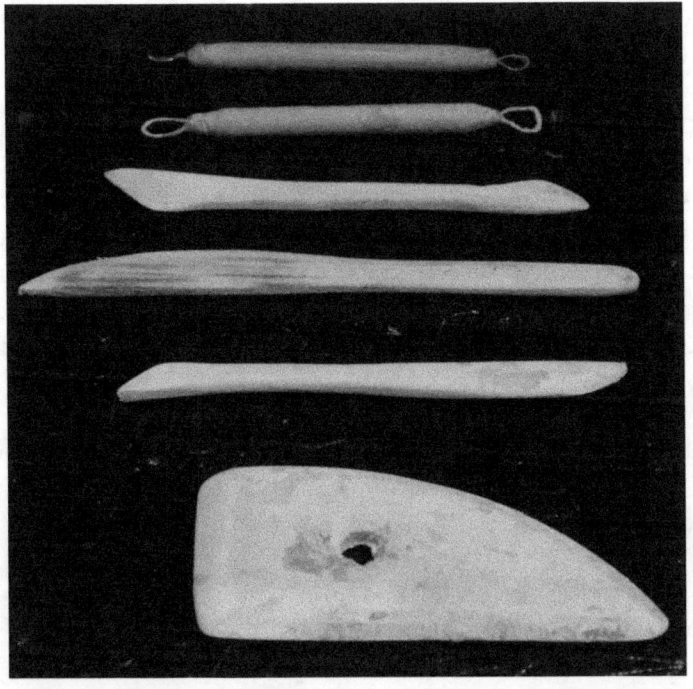

STEP 2: MAKING YOUR SCULPTING TOOLS

You don't have to listen to me on this one, and I'm betting most of you probably won't. But here's my rant anyway: *please* don't buy your sculpting tools. Try making them instead. The clay doesn't care what's pushing or poking it, so why pay extra for fancy materials and fancier brand names when you can make your own tools dirt cheap out of practically anything? (Especially when that money would be much better spent on more clay, plaster, and other supplies.)

Plus—and this can be very important for some projects—if you make your own tools then you can create special ones that will carve or impress unique textures into the clay, resulting in sculpts that are distinctly your own.

Most professional sculptors make their own tools. I personally enjoy doing it, not necessarily because of the price, but because of the craftsmanship. Call it a bonding moment between me and the artisans of the past. There is something about a handmade tool that makes me appreciate the work more. And I am using scraps that would otherwise end up in a landfill. So, by making my tools, I am satisfying a connection to the past and doing my best to stay as green as possible.

The patterns for the tools I most commonly use can be found at the following link www.russadams.me/toolpatterns. If you want to make them for yourself, here's how:

Begin by printing the patterns out on your printer. They should fit onto one page. You may need to adjust the size, but it's not likely. Cut the paper patterns out. Try to stay as close to the lines as possible.

Wooden Tools

Materials

1. ¼" thick piece of wood
2. Pattern

Tools

1. Scroll saw
2. Sandpaper
3. Dremel

Once you cut out the patterns, trace them onto any reasonably flat piece of wood about 1/4" thick. Then cut the raw shapes out. I use Cracker Barrel Cheddar boxes to make my wooden tools. My mother-in-law unloaded a ton of them on me a couple years back, and I have been slowly breaking them down as tool stock. I even use them when I make tools for the students that take my Latex Mask Making and Latex Puppet Making workshops.

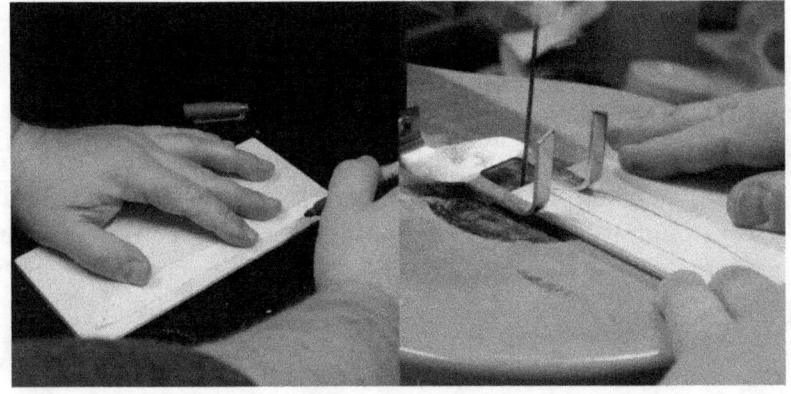

DIAGRAM 4

Once you have cut out your tools, put on your goggles and a dust mask and use a sander to smooth and refine the shapes indicated by the dashed lines in the drawings. A good Dremel tool with a sanding head or stone attachment works very well for this. Some of you may want to draw guidelines on the wood itself before starting, to help you control how much material you remove, and where you take it from.

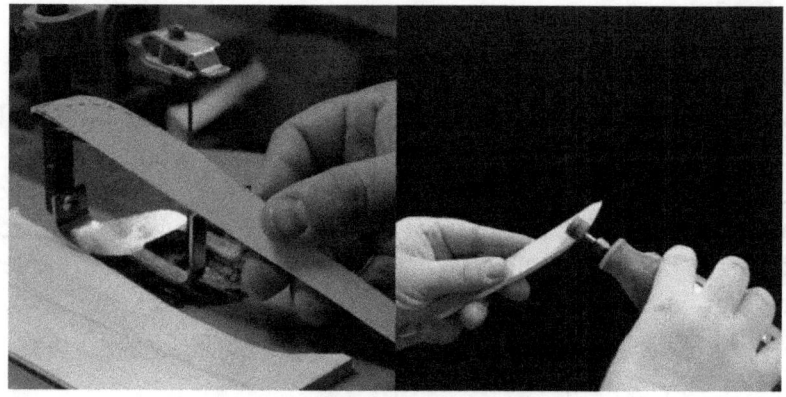

DIAGRAM 5

Of course, you don't have to make your sculpting tools out of wood if you don't want to. You can use metal, plastic, or even fiberglass. You simply need solid material in your hand. It should be firm enough to move the clay without bending or flexing. But remember that you may need to change how you cut and shape it depending on the material.

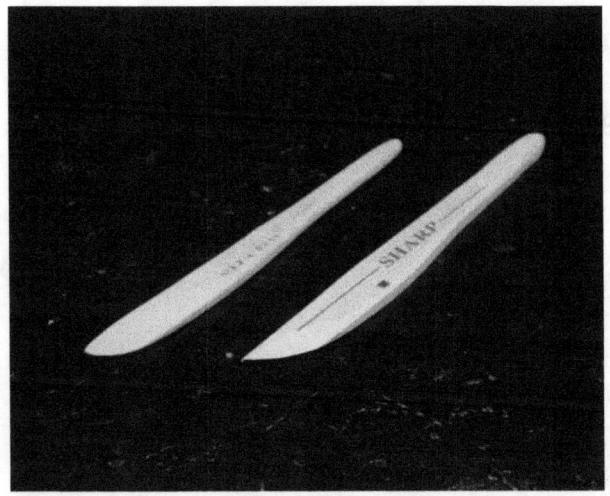

DIAGRAM 6

Rake Tools

Materials

1. Armature wire
2. Jeweler's wire
3. Masking tape
4. Plumbers epoxy
5. 3/8" dowel
6. Superglue
7. 5 Minute epoxy

Tools

1. Dremel
2. Drill
3. Pliers

A rake isn't as hard to make as you might think. There are a couple ways you can make these. The most common way to use a broken band-saw blade. But I am going to show a method I use. I like to use jeweler's wire and some simple baling wire to create mine. Depending on the size of the loop, I cut a six-inch length of baling wire and nine to twelve inches of jeweler's wire. The gauge doesn't really matter as long as it's pretty stiff stock.

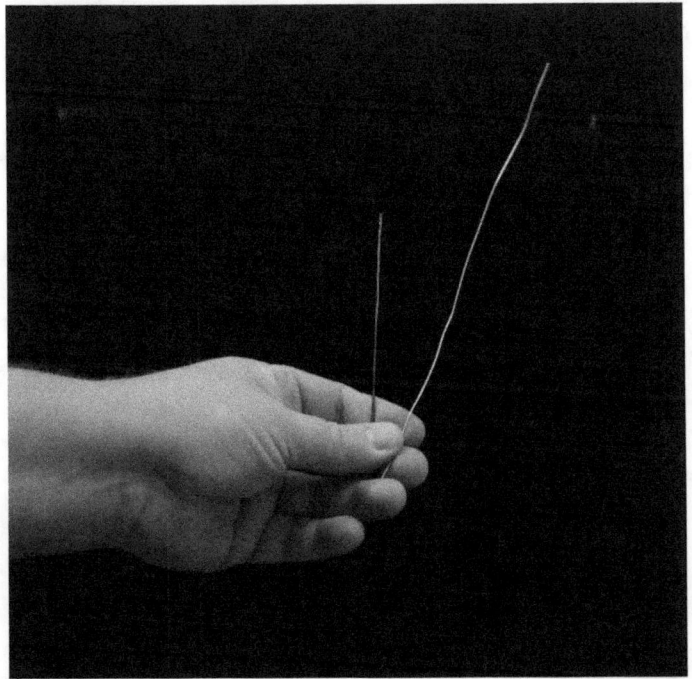

DIAGRAM 7

You want to give yourself a bit of space on either end of the baling wire; about an inch will do. At the inch mark, start coiling the jeweler's wire around the baling wire. Use Diagram 8 to guide you.

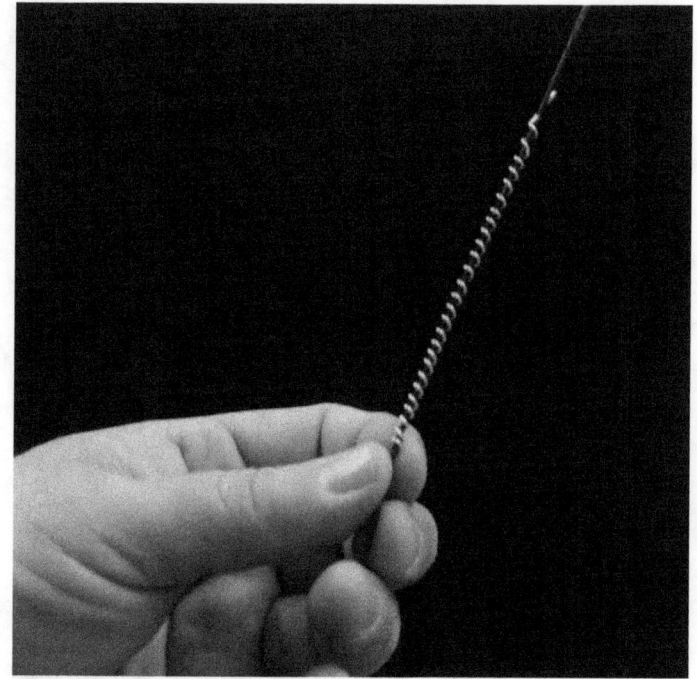

DIAGRAM 8

Gently, so as not to break the wire, make a series of bends in the wire to create an Omega symbol. Use the diagram below as an example.

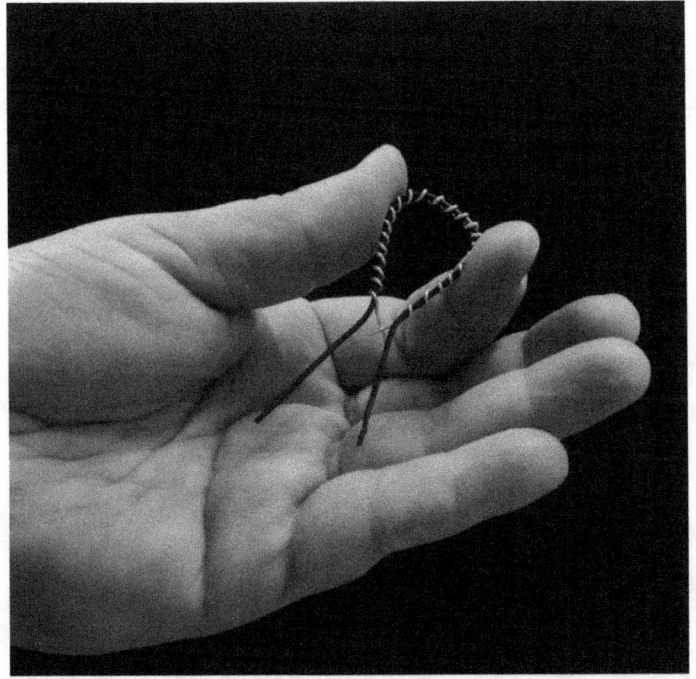

DIAGRAM 9

Cut a three-eighths dowel to a length of five or six inches. At one of the dowel, you will drill a hole using a drill bit that will produce a hole large enough to accommodate both ends of the baling wire. Make sure the wire is centered in the dowel. I suggest using a vise to stabilize the wooden dowel while you drill. You want to drill at least an inch into the dowel.

Test-fit the baling wire to 1) see that it fits, and 2) determine whether or not you need to trim any excess wire. When you insert the baling wire ends into the dowel, you want it to go in far enough for the jeweler's wire to touch the end of the dowel.

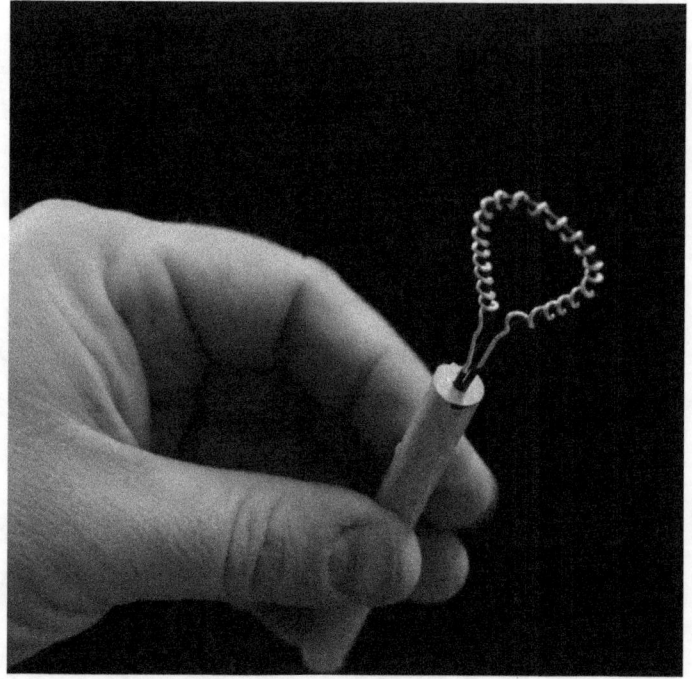

DIAGRAM 10

When this is accomplished, remove the wire and add a drop of superglue into the hole. Squeeze the ends of the wire together and reinsert them until the jeweler's wire stops at the dowel. Once the glue has had a chance to dry, use some plumber's epoxy to hold the pieces together.

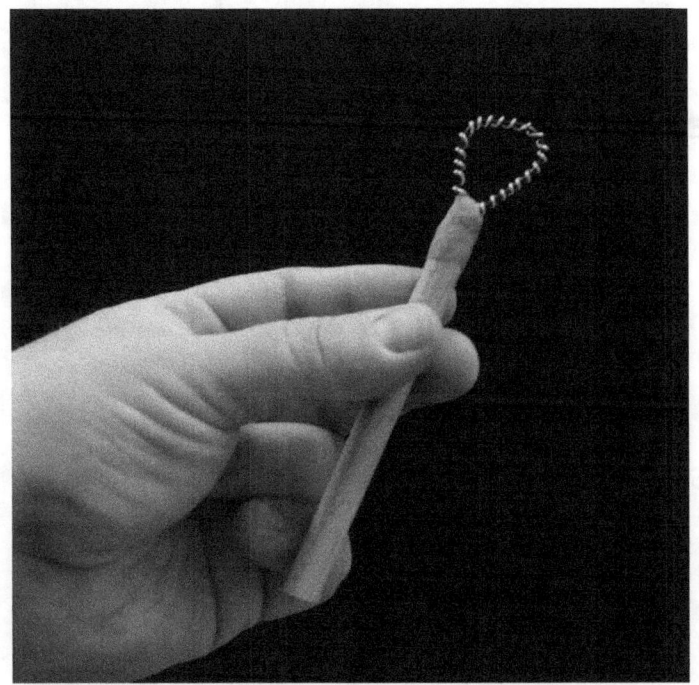

DIAGRAM 11

Loop Tools

Materials

1. Baling or armature wire
2. Masking tape
3. Plumbers epoxy
4. 3/8" dowel
5. Superglue
6. 5 Minute epoxy

Tools

1. Drill
2. Small drill bit
3. Clamp or vise

A loop tool is very simple to make as well. A three-eighths inch wood dowel cut to five or six inches will serve as the handle. A piece of baling wire or stiff jewelry wire will work for the loop. I would use heavier gauge wire for larger loop tools and small, but stiff, jeweler's wire for smaller loop tools. The larger tool would be used for blocking and rough detailing, while the smaller tool would be used for the finer detail. In addition to this larger tool, I also made a small and a micro version.

Drill a hole in the end of the dowel to accommodate the wire. The wire will be bent, so the hole you drill will have to accommodate both ends of the wire.

 Add a drop of superglue in the hole, and insert the two ends of the wire and you are set. I personally would add some five-minute epoxy or plumber's epoxy to the area where the wire meets the dowel as an added measure to hold the wire in place.

The wire might come out of the dowel from time to time. It sucks, but it does. Just put the wire back in the dowel with some glue. This is going to happen to you with just about any loop tool you buy as well. In this case, you made a tool rather than purchase one with the same defect.

NOTE: You can also scrap the wood dowel and use the plumber's epoxy to make the handle. This makes a better loop and rake tool. In this case, you cut your wire or blade about ten to twelve inches long and fold it in half (you will still need to grind the teeth on the blade). Use some masking tape to tightly hold about four inches of the wire together. Roll out some plumber's epoxy and cover the end of the wire in it to about the five-inch mark. Let it set. Once the epoxy kicks (or sets) you are ready to go.

Turntable (Lazy Susan)

Materials

1. Turntable bearing (Home Depot)
2. 2 12"x 12" pieces of wood
3. Wood screws

Tools

1. Drill
2. 1/2 or ¾" drill bit
3. Phillips head screwdriver
4. Scroll saw (or similar)
5. Black marker
6. Straight edge

Why a turntable? Like any tool, this one will make your life easier. You are going to need to turn your sculpture around to work on different sides. The weight of the clay can make turning it a pain, and you'll be turning it a lot. In fact, one of the effective methods I have found to regulate symmetry is to quickly turn the sculpture from right to left to observe how things like ears, jaw lines, and temple bones line up with each other. Try doing that without a turntable and you will quickly learn that having one makes life a whole lot easier.

Building one is simple. Again, you want to use scrap wood when possible. No point buying something that might be lying around in the garage. I am going to suggest you build a turntable that is twelve inches square. It's a good solid size and will accommodate large and small sculptures and armatures.

First thing, cut the two pieces of plywood, or whatever you have lying around. Try to keep the thickness of the wood to a reasonable measurement. Half an inch is good, three-quarters of an inch is good, but one-quarter inch is way too thin and an inch thick is overkill.

Once you have both of your twelve-inch pieces of wood cut out, you are going to want to find the center of both. The easiest way to do this is to line up a straight edge with opposite corners. I am using a yardstick. You will see an example of this in the diagram below. Line up the corners and draw a black line connecting them. Repeat this with the opposing corners. You will have a big black "X" on you the wood. The center of the wood square is where the lines intersect.

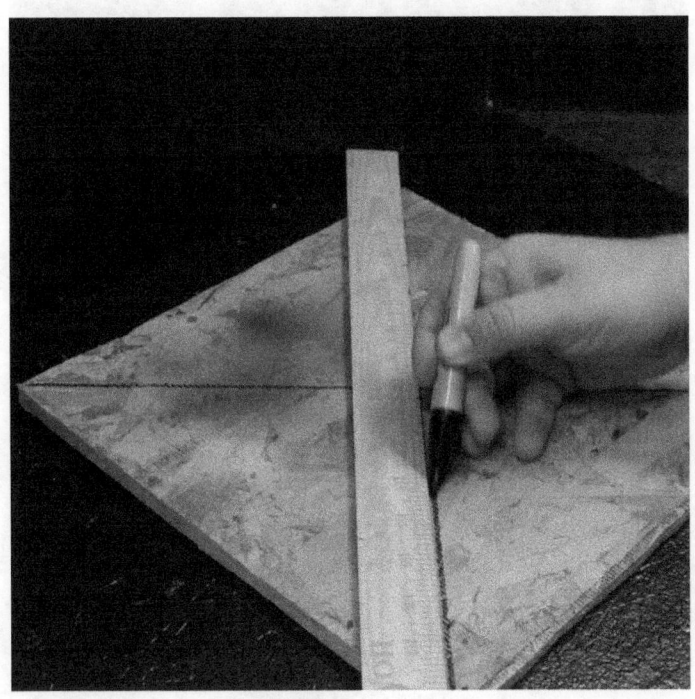

DIAGRAM 12

Next, take your turntable bearing and one of the twelve-inch wood plates and center it over that "X" you drew. You will see in the diagram I provided below that there are four corners on my turntable bearing. Mark those with a black marker. I mark them in case the bearing slides or moves when I am working. Next, use the wood screws to mount the bearing in place. The top level of the bearing should move freely.

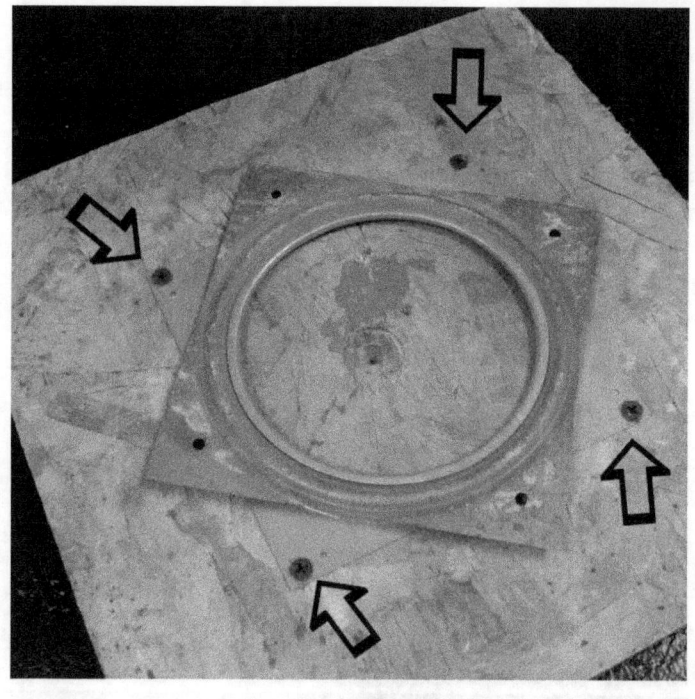

DIAGRAM 13

NOTE: There is a chance your wood screws are longer than the twelve-inch wood piece is thick. When you screw those into the wood, there may be barbs protruding from the back. You will need to grind them down to prevent them from hurting you, and from damaging your armature or items you place on top of the turntable. Use a Dremel or grinding wheel to work them down. This will heat up the screws. Use a spray bottle of water to take the heat out of it.

You may have to do this with side two of the turntable as well. ALWAYS WEAR EYE PROTECTION AND OTHER SAFETY GEAR.

Now look at Diagram 14. I have turned the bearing so the points of the top plate are centered between the screw holes of the lower plate. It should look like an octagon or eight-pointed star. It doesn't matter which of the top plate corners you choose, but choose one and mark the hole with a marker. Then use your half-inch or three-quarter-inch drill bit to drill out that point. This is the access hole you will use to mount the other twelve-inch piece of wood to the bearing.

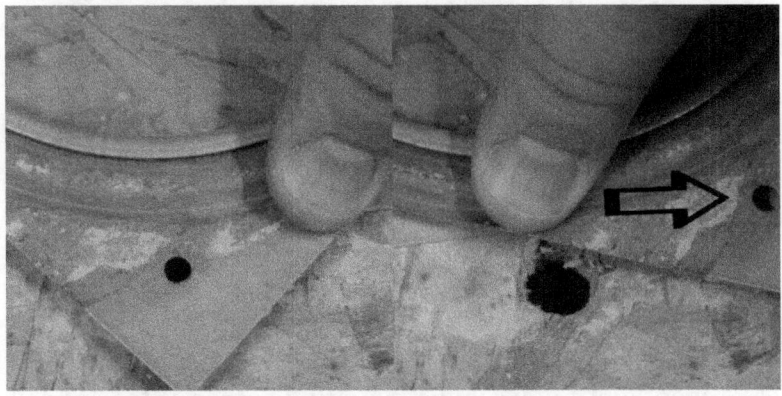

DIAGRAM 14

Once you have the access hole drilled out, place the second twelve-inch piece of wood on top of the bearing. Try your best to make sure the two pieces of wood line up. Set the turntable down with the UNATTACHED piece of wood down on your work surface. You want the access hole on top as shown in Diagram 15.

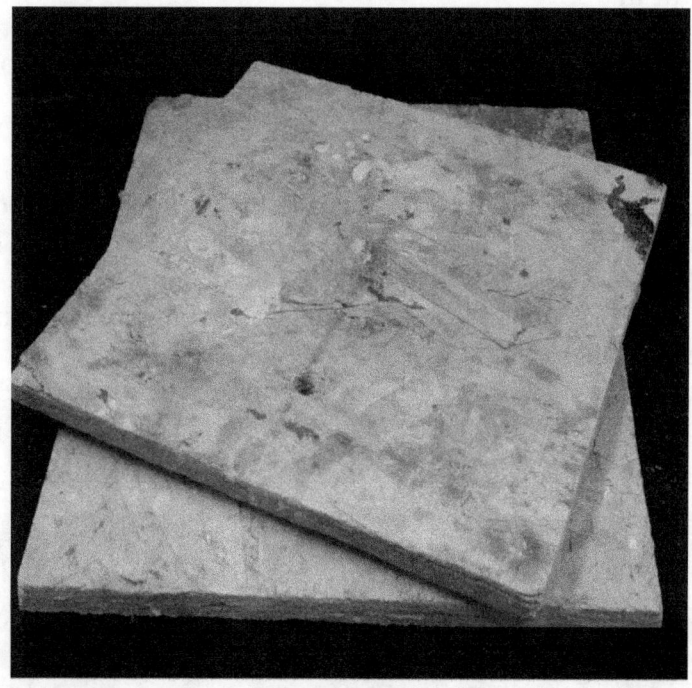

DIAGRAM 15

Looking through the access hole, turn the top (or MOUNTED) piece of wood until you see the mounting corner of the opposite bearing plate. This is shown in Diagram 16.

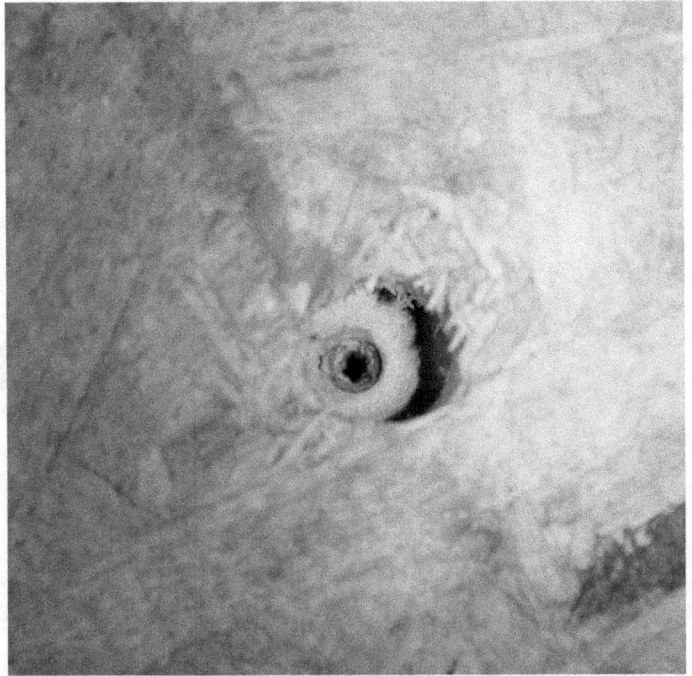

DIAGRAM 16

In Diagram 16, I drilled a pilot hole for the first wood screw. You don't need to do this. It was mainly to illustrate where the wood screw will go. Using a Phillips head screwdriver and a wood screw, get that corner of the plate mounted. Then, repeat this until all four corners of the bearing are mounted to the lower piece of wood. See Diagram 17.

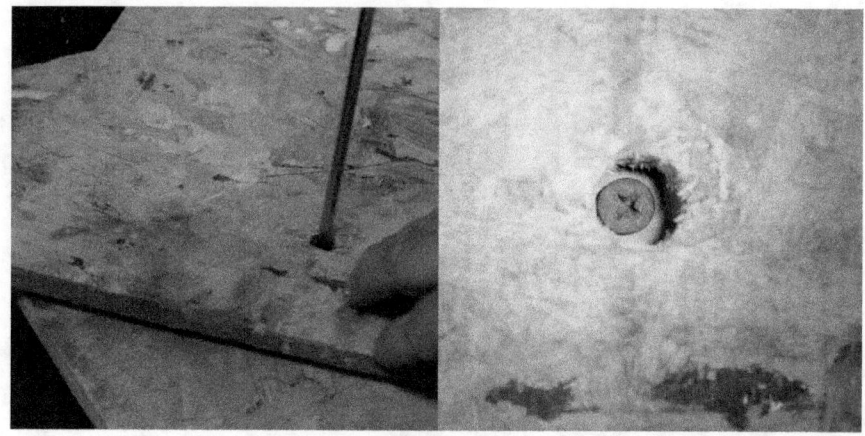

DIAGRAM 17

Congrats, you have just added another important piece to your sculpting tools and you probably spent between five to ten dollars. Not including shipping, I have seen turntables for as low as thirty dollars in art catalogs and as high as one-hundred-fifty dollars. This one will last years if you take care of it, and you can use the money you saved to buy more clay and plaster.

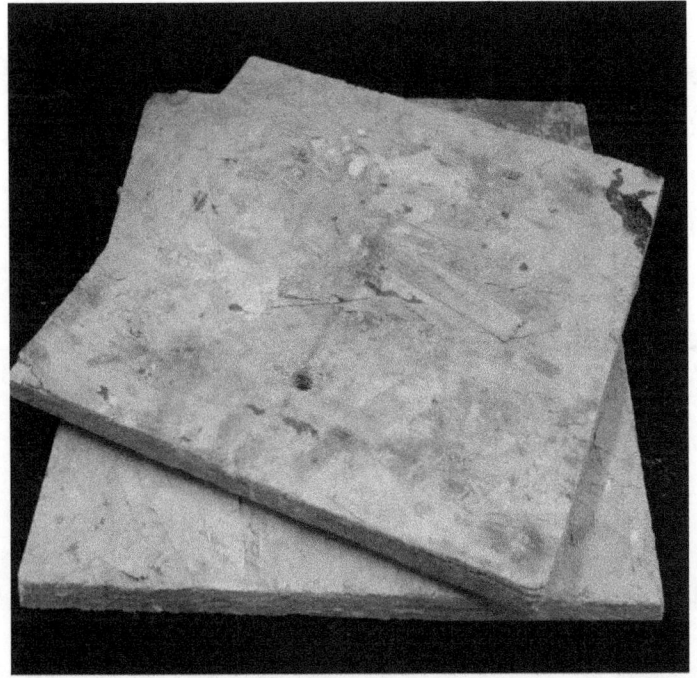

FINISHED TURNTABLE

Once you have tools—whether you made them or bought them—
you are ready to start sculpting.

Russ Adams

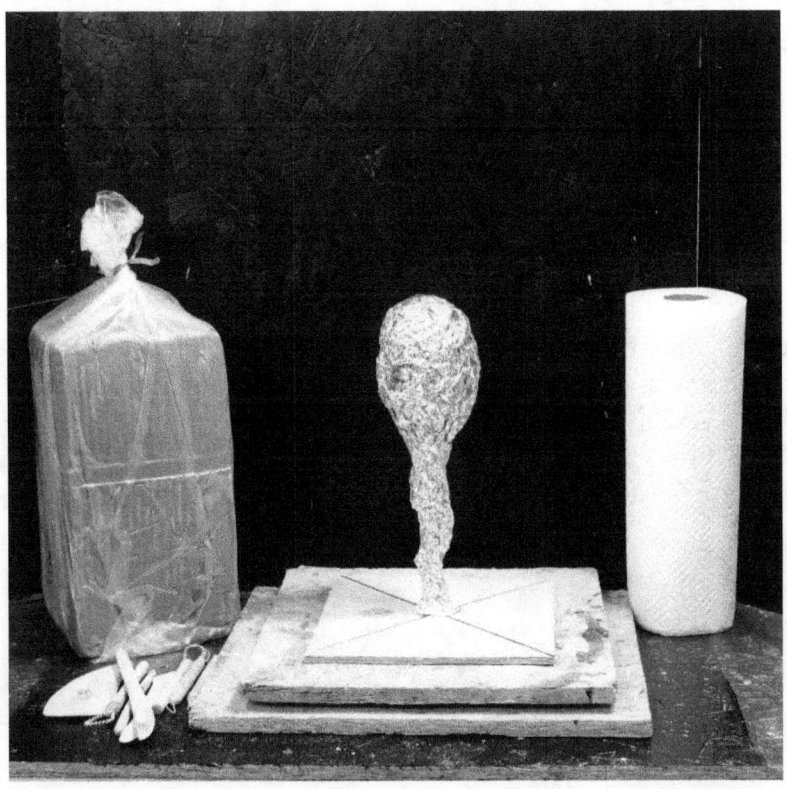

STEP 3: SCULPTING

Sculpting Materials

1. WED Clay (Not WET clay)
2. Paper towels
3. Plastic trash bag
4. Clear matte spray paint (Krylon Clear Acrylic Spray)
5. Reference materials

Russ Adams

Tools

1. Chip brush
2. A spray bottle for water
3. Sculpting tools
4. The armature
5. Turntable (Lazy Susan)

We are going to start by evenly covering the foil head of the armature with clay. You want to make sure the head is totally covered in clay. The reason for this is we don't want the foil poking through the clay. It's unsightly, obstructive, and when we mold, the plaster can escape down a foil rabbit hole and cause havoc.

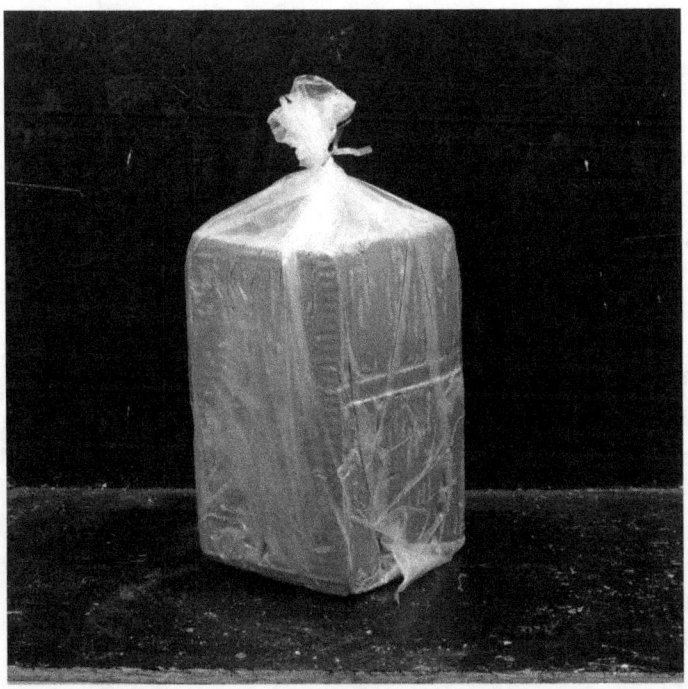

WED CLAY

As I have previously mentioned, we are going to be using WED Clay for this project, but you can use whatever clay you like. WED Clay is a water-base clay hybrid that includes a glycerin additive that slows the drying process. I am certain this is a gross generalization of the product, but it gets the point across to those of us lacking a degree in chemistry.

This clay is also an industry standard so you are likely to see many professional artists using it both in their shops and their tutorials. One of the most beautiful things about WED, besides the immensely low price tag, is the clay's durability. WED will dry out if left to do so. It is water based, hybrid or not. But it can be rejuvenated, even when it's completely dried out. It takes time, a lot of time, but I have done it on several occasions.

When I am done using this clay, I toss it into a five-gallon bucket with a wet sponge—maybe some extra water depending on how dry it is—and leave it sit for a few weeks and BOOM...I have my clay back.

This same method works if the clay is completely dried out. Put the clay into a bucket with about an inch or two of water. Seal the lid and let it sit for a few weeks. It takes longer to reconstitute it, but it will eventually return to its original state. My advice is to put the clay in a bucket right after you're done using it. Seal it up with a damp cloth or sponge and set it aside for later.

I have eight five-gallon buckets of WED waiting to be used, and they have been sitting in my shop for years. So, it's not like once it dries out it's gone, but let's not mistreat it in the first place.

The other thing I love about this clay is its workability. Water knocks down surfaces and smooths it like glass. On the other hand, you can use a heat gun or torch and cook the surface and scratch in some extremely fine details like crow's feet, or willowing wrinkles like those fine features seen in the faces of the elderly. If the clay layer is thick enough, eventually it will feed moisture back to the surface and the area that was torched or cooked will return to its softer state after a short time, all the while leaving behind the wonderful details that had been created.

Most people might think a water based clay would force you to mold quickly after sculpting, but that's not true with WED. You can cover the sculpture with damp paper towels and a plastic bag and leave the sculpture for weeks. Although I don't recommend it.

About a year ago, I was working on a large sculpture, and I ran out of time. I had a string of appearances at comic cons around the country and when I returned I just knew my sculpture was trashed. It had been sitting on the workbench for nearly two months. I took the bag off, and notice the paper towels I used to wrap the sculpture were still a little damp—sporting some mildew, but still damp. When I removed them, I was thrilled—astonished—to find my sculpture was 100% ready and waiting for me to continue working.

Ok, I am going to stop my infomercial for WED Clay. I love this stuff.

Design

We need to focus for a minute on design. What design concept do you want? Are you going for realism, caricature, cute, or gross? There is no right or wrong answer but you should have that in your mind before you start. It's not a good idea to switch gears in the middle of a project, though it does happen. Having a design plan in mind keeps you focused on the end goal.

I have a few caricature versions of my shrunken heads: Spock, Vincent Price, Danny Trejo, etc. I also have semi-realistic shrunken heads that are very popular. I also have hyper-realistic shrunken heads, some latex and some silicone. I like to change it up from time to time. The point is people love shrunken heads, for whatever twisted reason. Whether yours is realistic or cartoon-like, it's going to be a hit.

I am going to focus on realism in this workshop, which is to say much of my sculpting tutorial will focus on creating a realistic-looking shrunken head. The basic information is the same if you are doing a caricature design of a famous person. The only difference between mine and yours is that you will most likely need to include bone structure, so that you can pull off a shrunken head that resembles a famous person.

Keep this in mind, the main esthetic in design with shrunken heads is uneven shrinkage. You never really know how the skin will shrink from victim to victim. Even the process or methodology will affect the outcome. With that said, you have a great deal of freedom in your project.

Basically, you can follow along and try to copy my progress or feel free to deviate. With the design in mind we can move on to collecting reference materials.

Reference Photo

Reference photos are a major contributor to a successful project, whether it's sculpting, painting, or furring a creature. Humans sometime add or change elements in their mind's eye that are nothing like our subjects. We all know what a skull looks like. We are bombarded with them almost daily. Movies, tattoos, drawings, advertising, cartoons, etc.—they seem to be everywhere.

If you were asked to draw or sculpt a skull from memory there would be a lot of missing details, added information, or distortions. Certainly, if you showed that drawing or sculpture to people they would immediately see a skull, but it may lean toward a cartoon, have a facial expression, or look like a Picasso. You will do a much better job of drawing or sculpting that skull if you have references in front of you.

It's always important to have something to refer to even if your creature or character is completely fabricated in your imagination. Even an imaginary character has elements based in reality—feathers, hair, teeth, body shapes, etc.

I like to have my bases covered when I am sculpting. I like to have those elements in front of me to refer to so I don't mistakenly veer off track. I look for as many angles as I can in my reference. Profiles, straight-on shots, the top of the head, and the bottom--I grab whatever I can.

I need to be clear, you are not copying these images. You are using them as a guide to ground you in the reality of the character or creature you are making. They are a guide. So, you aren't cheating by using materials that most special-effects artists use. I would say all special-effects artists. There is always one person out there that just has to say, "Well I don't. Never have never will." There is always one.

My advice is to do a Google search for "shrunken heads." Click on Google Images and print the photos that closely resemble the design you most want to incorporate into your shrunken head. Make sure you get lots of angles. My favorite references come from unpainted or raw photos, like "In Progress" Z-Brush photos. Often the paint and hair can hide details and structure. I want to see those, so many of my reference images lack paint and décor. That said, I also want to see images that do have paint schemes, decor, or hair styles that I will incorporate into my project after I have molded and cast it. But, that's for later, during the finishing stage.

I will repeat this later, but ALWAYS print your references. We are going to be making a horrible mess during this process and you absolutely don't want your electronic devices becoming a causality.

Blocking

What is blocking? Have you ever seen a sketch in progress? The illustrator begins by sketching out these crazy geometric shapes that look like they could never possibly turn in a sexy comic book vixen, but you know they will. Blocking is when sculptors lay out geometric-like shapes, which later turn into that sexy vixen, basically. Only our vixen is going to have her head lopped off, the skin peeled off and… You know what? I am just going to stop there.

When a sculptor "block outs" a form, he/she is really just slapping big chunks of clay onto the sculpture to create simplified forms, which will be worked in stages.

In the blocking stage, you build up masses of clay to create structure, then smooth them down with a spatula, rake tool, or loop tool. We will add clay to build up the shape of the brow, the crown of the head, the jaw, the nose, the cheeks, and the back of the head. It's going to look primitive as you work, but don't freak out—by definition blocking is not pretty, so don't get frustrated if your results look crude.

Look at my progress. You will see mine looks similar to yours. See Diagram 18.

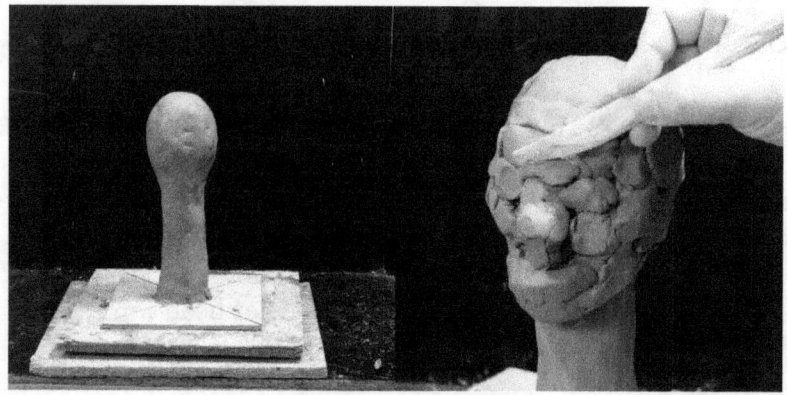

DIAGRAM 18

And don't be in a hurry. Whenever I teach sculpting classes, I always have to tell my students to slow down and not rush ahead. Skipping a step in the sculpture process often means having to destroy what was prematurely created and starting up again because the form wasn't quite right. To keep you from repeating your efforts, I want you to slow down. Plus, sculpting is meditative. So, chill!

As you work to complete the rough shape of your sculpture, keep checking in with your reference material. I cannot stress how important it is, especially starting out, to have pictures on hand to look at.

> **PRO TIP:** While sculpting, do *not* try and use your phone, iPad, or computer as a way to look at reference pictures. Print them out instead. Some clays (like WED Clay) dry on your fingers and leave an abrasive material that will scratch the crap out of your device screens. And who needs dried clay flakes or dust getting behind buttons

of your computer's keyboard? That will certainly muck things up.

So, take it easy on your electronics and yourself—*print out your reference images*. Don't waste them either, even if they get trashed during use. You'll probably want to use them again. I keep mine organized in folders for easy access. Let's be green about it…as much as we can be.

Once you have created the mass you're happy with, start roughing out the eyes, the location of the nose, and the mouth.

It's natural for you to want to add things like cheek bones, the orbital bones around the eyes, temple bones, and even the nasal bone, but don't. The two things these features have in common are:

1) they are bones, and

2) they aren't there in a shrunken head.

Remember, someone took the skin off the skull and probably tossed the bones to the village dog, and I don't mean the chieftain's daughter. Too far? Anyway, there are no cheek bones because they can't shrink a skull. You can play with these areas but they shouldn't be predominant.

Scoop out the cheeks or fatten them up depending on how much or little straw the practitioner used to stuff the head.

The same can be said for the eyelids. There is no eyeball to hold them in the hemisphere shape, but there is a lot of skin there and as it shrinks the eye area could become puffy or totally go the other way and appear sunken in. For now, let's jam some clay in there as a place holder. We will talk more about that in a second.

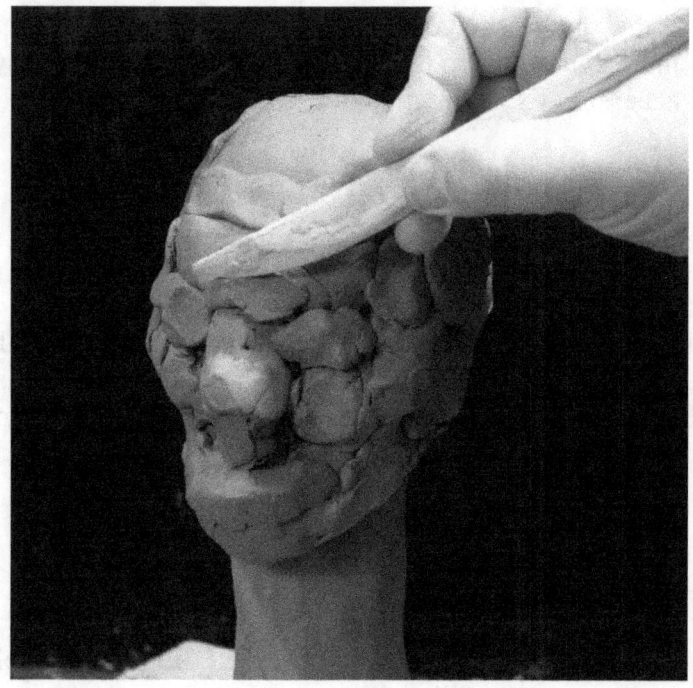

DIAGRAM 19

One feature that is likely missing but needs to be present for this project is the neck. We need to have a neck for our sculpture. Why? We need it because when we make the mold: this neck will actually become the tube into which we pour the liquid latex. So, it's necessary, but you won't need to detail it. When we finally get to the latex shrunken head that comes out of the mold, we will cut off the head at the neck, just like the head-shrinking practitioner did. Creepily similar, ain't it?

Shrunken Heads

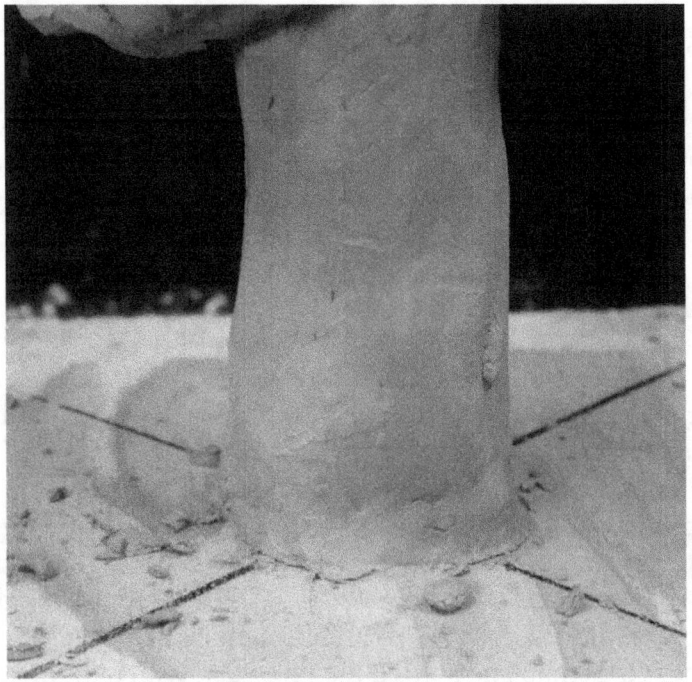

DIAGRAM 20

Once we have all that blocking done, we can move on to the next phase of sculpting, the Rough Detailing.

Rough Detail

Rough detailing is where we knock down the mass of clay we used in the blocking process. You will be using a rake or loop tool more often here than most other tools in this step. Use your larger rake tool to gently knock down the blocking and transform it into a more recognizable surface--still raw, but appearing more refined than in the blocking stage.

At the end of the blocking phase I mentioned the lack of bones in the face. This is where we can play into that vacancy by either creating deep recesses or fattening them up—again depending on how your imaginary practitioner fills the head with straw. Perhaps this practitioner was new to the job. Maybe he forgot to pack the head with straw and just hung the face sack on a stick, which would result in the depression. If that is the case, gravity would have played upon the skin, like a clock in a Salvador Dali painting. Or perhaps he stuffed the face sack with a lot of straw, which might over plump the head. It's all about your vision.

Do make sure to remove the appearance of bone as much as you can if you are following me in my development of a realistic shrunken head. The jawline will no longer be defined, nor is the brow ridge, or chin. You can, however, build a mass of skin.

Fatten up that nose. Think of the mass of skin there. It's pretty thick so it would have less shrinkage and appear bulbous. Same with the ears. They are mostly cartilage, and that fatty earlobe would have remained large too.

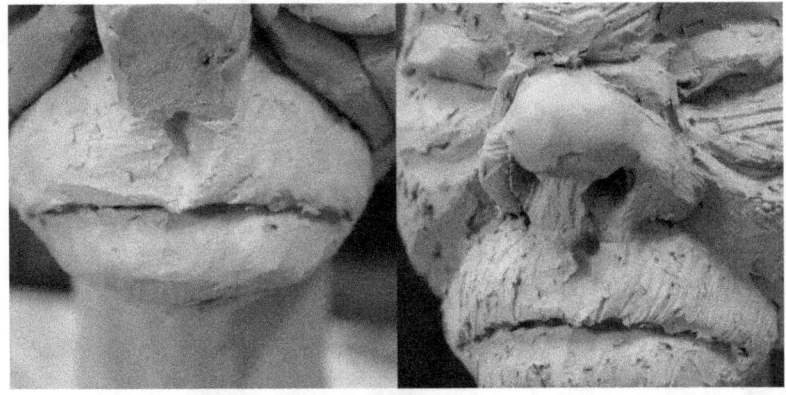

DIAGRAM 21

I like to sculpt the rough ears side by side on my workspace—not on the sculpture. I do this because I can make both ears the same size, shape, and detail. Once I am done, I will add them to the sculpture. Once they are on the sculpture, then I will start working on the finer details…when we get to that step, of course.

It really beats having to switch from one side of the face to the other simply to eyeball the other ear I sculpted. Even then, the size and shape may not be consistent. Give it a try and see if it works for you. I have included a diagram below showing how I lay out the process of creating a rough ear.

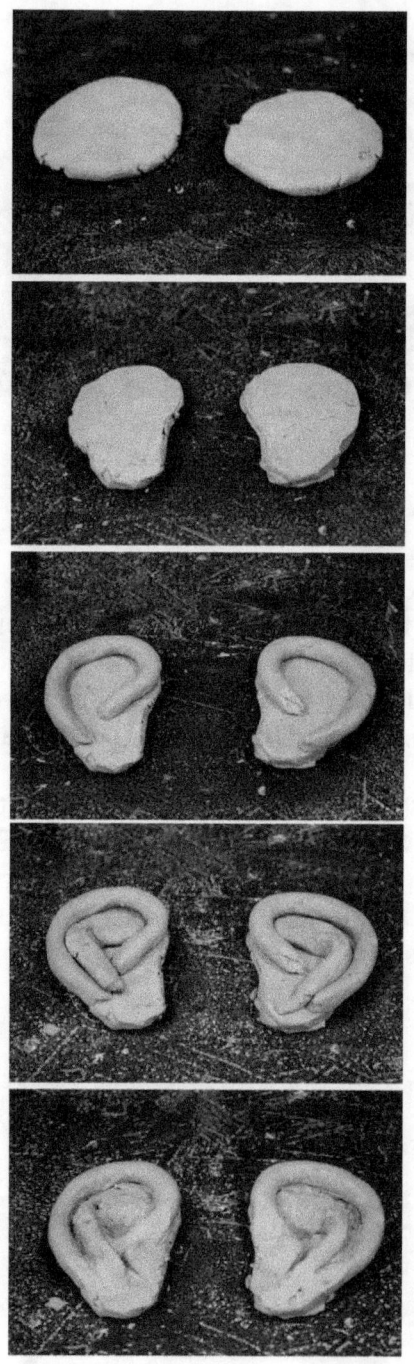

The lips would have been huge and pouty. Perhaps that lower lip juts out much farther than it had before this fella's mutilation.

Along with the missing jawline, that chin would disappear or at most be a knot of flesh. That lower lip might be more predominant if the chin was missing. If the shrunken head victim was fat, there might have been so much skin that he had a bullfrog-looking mass under that chin.

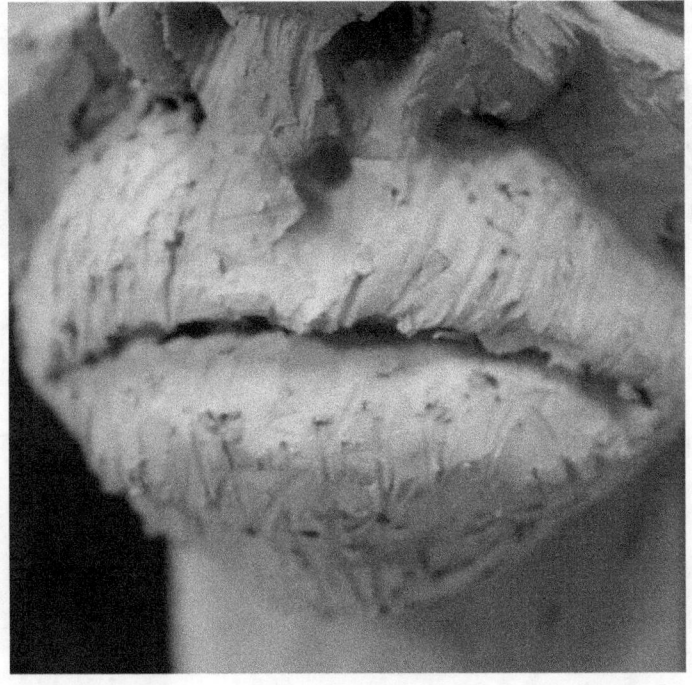

DIAGRAM 22

Once you have defined these features, round them off using the rake or loop tools. Gently knock down the edges. You should round off all the areas of the head, front and back. There should be mild tool marks everywhere indicating that you have looked over every inch of this sculpture.

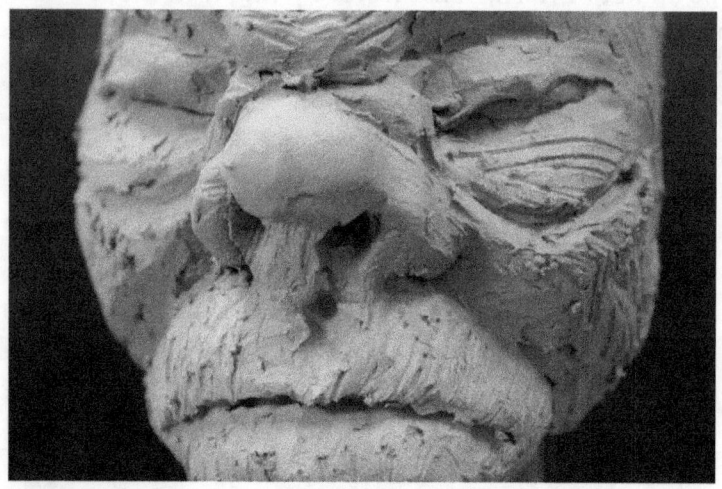

DIAGRAM 23

With that completed, we can move onto refining detail.

Refining Detail

Refining detail is just what the name suggests, refining the details. We will be using our spatula, the small rake tool, an ultra-small loop tool, and perhaps a toothpick to go over this sculpture.

Remember, anything goes. You are limited only by the concept of shrinkage. There may be deep-set pock marks on his nose and chin. Scars would be more predominant, and wrinkles might lessen—reversing time as it were.

For the sake of this book, let's start with the chin and work our way up and back. There are still going to be hairs on this chap's face, so we might need deep pores. Don't sculpt the hair. We are going to leave hair for the finishing work later in the book. Instead, we are going to pave the groundwork for those hairs. Think about the pores they are growing out of. Add as many as you like using that toothpick. Don't go too deep, just hit the surface. Then smooth out the area where the skin folds into the pores or holes. Don't simply make a hole in the face. Think of the divot in Kurt Douglas' chin—only ours will be smaller and there will be more than one. It's got to look natural.

Now grab a 1" chip brush, and cut the bristles off about half way. The bristles are now shorter and stiffer because you cut them off. Spritz some water on the area and massage the pores with the brush. Like I said earlier, water will break down the WED Clay.

Note:

Alcohol breaks down oil-based clay like Klean Clay

Water breaks down water-based clay like WED Clay

Russ Adams

> Solvents like acetone and paint thinner break down polymer clay like Chavant Clay
>
> Use eye protection and respirators when using these materials.

With a little water on the chip brush, gently work the bristles over the pores. If you accidently obliterate them, don't worry, just recreate the pores and start again. This process will smooth the surface and round the edges of the pores. This method can even be used to smooth wrinkles and bumps you put on the face.

Move up to the lips. There may still be cracks in the surface of the lips, but they will be rounded off as well. You can use that toothpick to carve deep and willowy lines into the lips. Perhaps the bottom lip split as a result of the moisture rapidly escaping the flesh. Maybe it's a nasty split, one that might get our practitioner into trouble with the spirits. It can be a nasty gash but it may need smoothing with that water and modified chip brush.

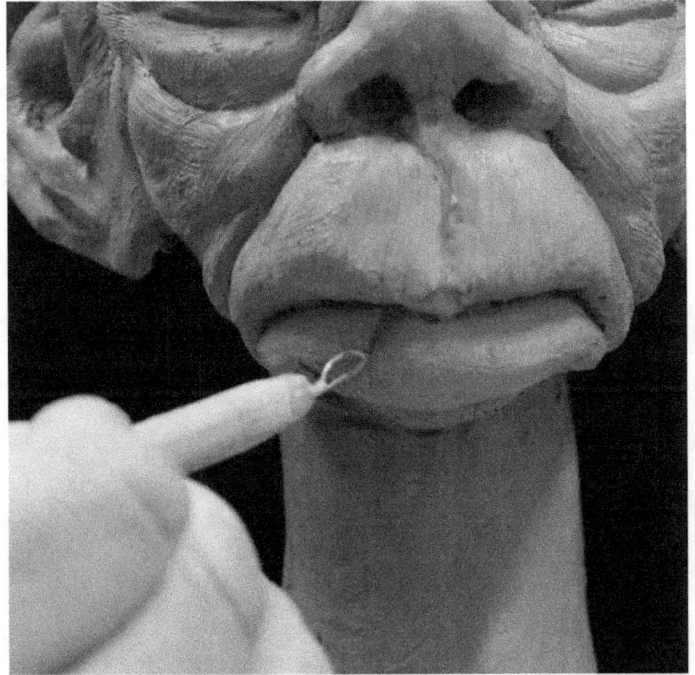

DIAGRAM 25

How do you want to treat the corners of the mouth? I say we puff them up by exaggerating the nasolabial folds and extend them to the corners of the mouth. It might also be a good idea to make the Philtrum (the ditch under your nose) a bit more pronounced.

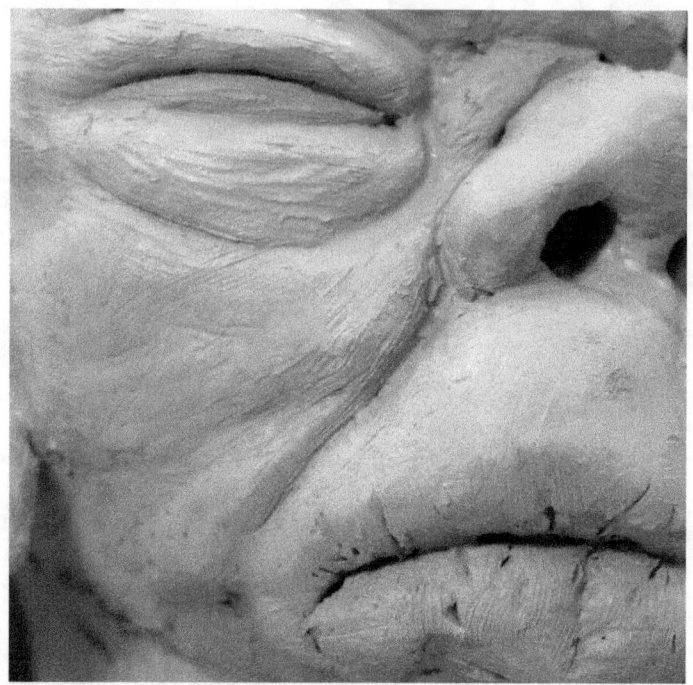

DIAGRAM 26

The nose itself can go the piggy direction, or maybe the mass fell forward and is more deflated than turned up. The main thing is that it should be large, fat, and bulbous. It's a good thick piece of flesh. It won't shrink down to a cute little button. Find a good reference that appeals to you, and replicate it. Keep in mind, it might have a smoother surface than the skin under the eyes.

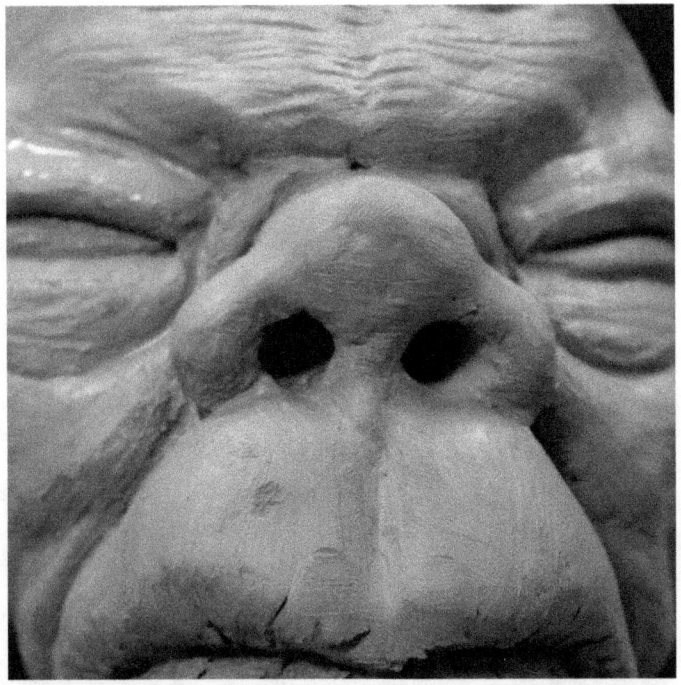

DIAGRAM 27

The skin on the bridge of the nose is thinner, and would shrink up more, which pulls the nose back to that piggy-like appearance. It might change your character's face and make it appear as if it's disgusted or irritated. Can you blame him?

The shrinking in this area might even result in a heavier brow—a huge roll of skin crashing down onto the bridge of the nose. Though it has shrunk, there might still be a smooth, shallow ditch that remains. You can use your spatula tool to carve a couple deep lines under the roll of skin so it looks more like a wave of flesh rolling toward the nose. Then take the modified chip brush and water, and softly erode the harder lines in the brow. Weather that area until it appears natural.

The brow is really just a wild card. It can be smooth and without detail, or it can be heavy and bumpy. There may not be a pronounced divot near the third eye area, but fleshy deposits might have collected there and might not have shrunk evenly. Again, it's a matter of design esthetics.

Remember when I mentioned uneven shrinkage being the esthetic of this project? The bridge of the nose and brow are prefect examples.

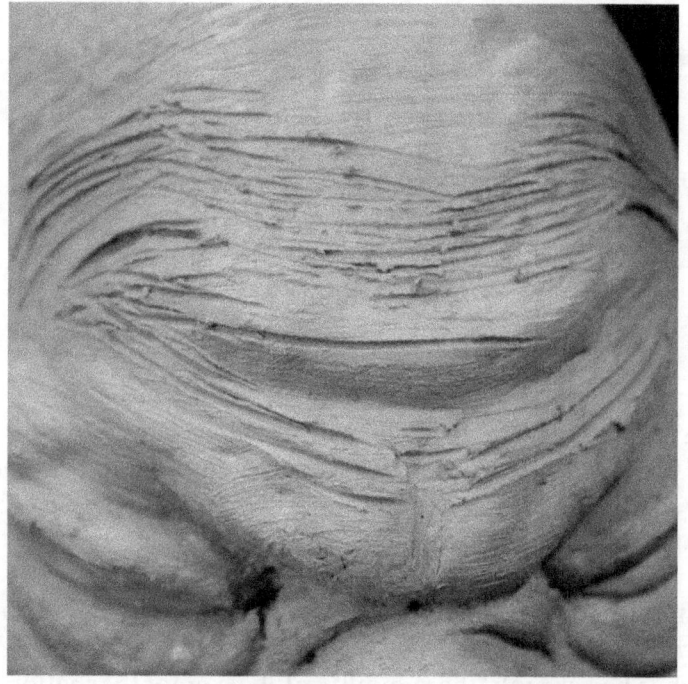

DIAGRAM 28

Do you see how your idea or vision of how the head was dried could transform a head in different ways?

When it comes to the eyelids, I always like to make them fat and puffy. Eyelids are so much thicker than people think. In fact, I often have to instruct my students to thicken up lids almost three times thicker than they envision them. These little sacks of skin won't puff up quite as much as the nose, but they will puff out. I like to add rolls of skin to both the upper and lower lids to make them look as if they are swollen. It's a personal choice and completely artistic. Because of the mass of skin in the eyelid, I think the fatty area might engulf or cover details like the tear duct. The same with the outer corner of the eyes.

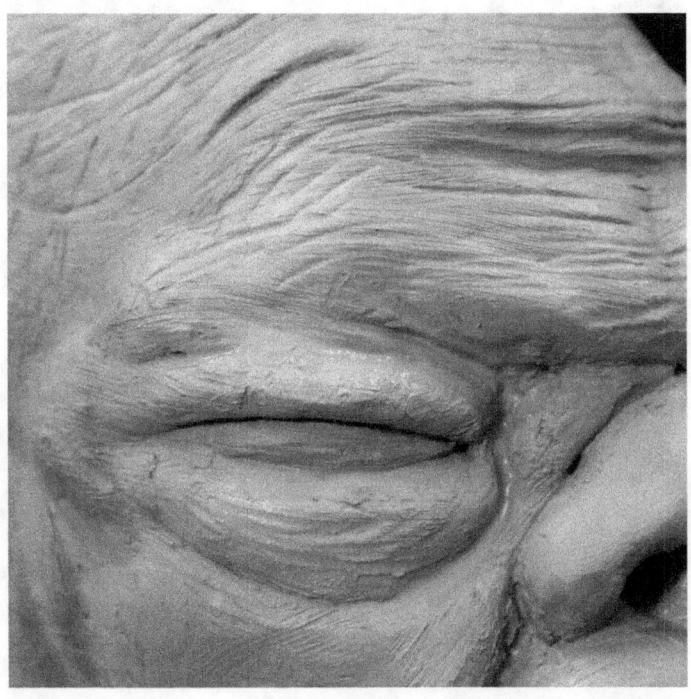

DIAGRAM 29

When it comes to the ears, they would remain larger. After all, it's not likely they would try to excise the cartilage like they did the skull. There might be some pronounced fatty deposits around the earlobe, and in front of the Crus of Helix (the area where the rim of the ear curves into the ear and stops above the ear canal). In fact, there might be a lot of material built up here. Bumpy, like a cluster of sebaceous cysts. Gross, but that is the point.

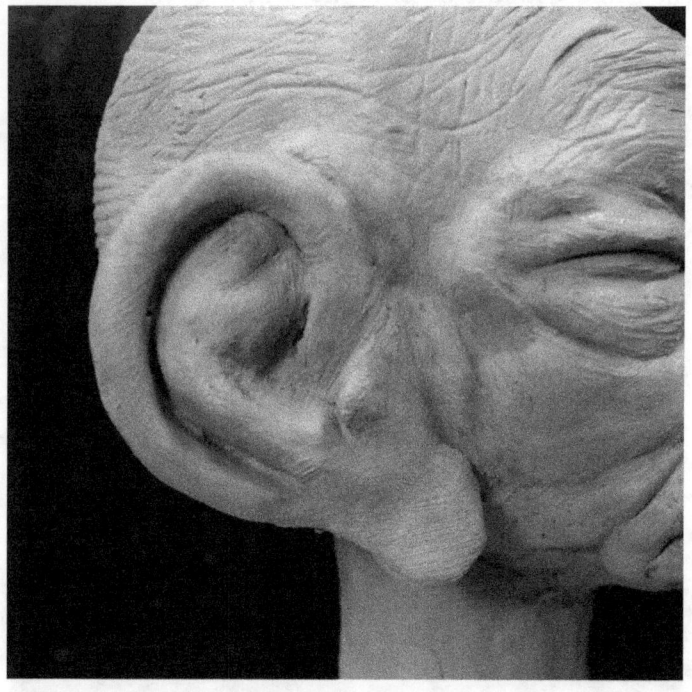

DIAGRAM 30

There are a few more things to consider. Veining is one of those considerations. Don't add them. Veins that present on the surface of the skin, like the stress veins that pop when your father is angry, aren't likely to be visible. Veins present like this because of muscle tension, bone, and vascular pressure. None of these will exist to cause this to happen. If you create them, you may be making a mistake.

Another mistake you might make is mass wrinkles. If the practitioner simply removed the head, and dried the skin, this might have amplified the process. But since the skin is boiled first, that seems to have plumped the skin with added water, such as when you boil a hotdog rather that microwave it. There might still be moderate wrinkling, but not a lot. Consult your references to be sure.

In place of wrinkles, you might instead see fine cracking in the surface of the skin. Imagine a ceramic coffee cup you have used for years. Look at all the stains trapped in the tiny network of cracks. I foresee this being most present on areas like the chin, tip of the nose, brow, and cheeks. They might even occur on the helix of the ears.

I would heat the surface of these areas one at a time with a heat gun or torch. Then use a finely-tipped tool like a toothpick to scratch in those ultra-fine details. Cook the surface of the clay a bit using a torch or a heat gun. It should look lighter than the surrounding clay when you're done. Don't go to crazy with this because you could crack the clay down to the armature. Just scratch the desired pattern into the surface. Be gentle. You want just enough pressure for your detail to be seen. You can use this method to create fine wrinkles as well.

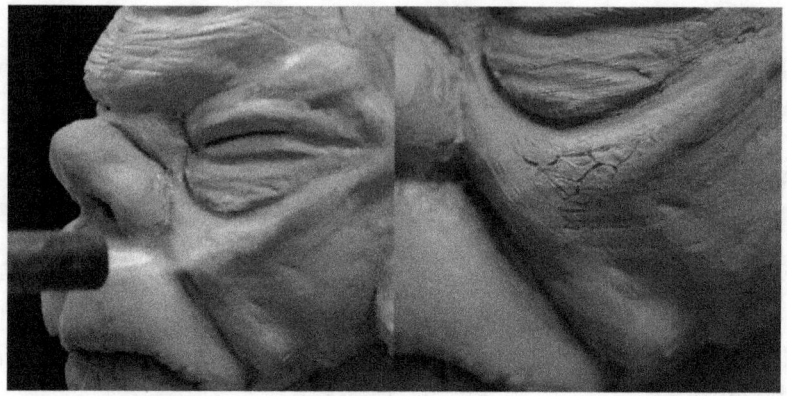

DIAGRAM 31

Again, these are all just suggestions to get you thinking about how you want to sculpt your project. The important thing is that you consider options and probabilities as you sculpt. Therefore, a good backstory helps you create. Only the backstory for this creation will have more to do with the practitioner, and little to do with the victim, because what the practitioner did, and his experience level, says a lot about the outcome of this whole thing.

Once you are comfortable with your sculpture, you can move on to the molding stage. If you don't have time to jump right into the molding stage, then drape some damp paper towels over the sculpture and cover that in a plastic bag. A couple plastic grocery bags should do the trick for a project this small. Just make sure you close off the opening of the bag to seal in the moisture. This will keep the project safe until you can mold.

> **PRO TIP:** I don't suggest waiting to mold your
> sculptures. The longer you wait the greater risk of
> damage. Forget, for a moment, that the WED Clay can,

and will, dry out. It is much more likely with smaller sculptures like a shrunken head. There just isn't enough clay there to retain water for a long period. That aside, there are a host of other issues that might come into the picture—things you might never think of. Crazy off-the-wall things that couldn't possibly happen…but do.

Back when my studio was a one-car-garage, I was working on a werewolf mask. I called it werewolf 1.0. Werewolf 1.0B was a big seller; in fact, Jimmy Fallon has a copy. Werewolf 1.0 never made an appearance. I loved this mask. I was so proud of it. I remember that I had been working on it for a week and I was exhausted afterward. I just couldn't face making a mold so soon after putting in all that work.

I put my tools down on a Friday and spent the weekend relaxing with my family. Monday rolled around and I felt refreshed, so refreshed that I decided to do other things. A friend of my wanted to go fishing on Tuesday, so I brushed it off again. Wednesday I was ready to go. Hell, I was even excited about molding.

I grabbed a cup of coffee and raced out to the garage…I mean studio. Turns out, there wouldn't be a mold that day either. One of the fluorescent lights, hood and all, had magically broken free and swung down, crashing into the sculpture. The fluorescent tube shattered and there was glass everywhere.

The damage to the sculpture wasn't horrible. But while I was cleaning up the mess the boom knocked into the table leg, and for whatever reason the leg collapsed and the sculpture hit the floor…that puppy was trashed.

The moral of this story is, you never know when fate is going to dog you. So, don't leave your sculpture longer than necessary.

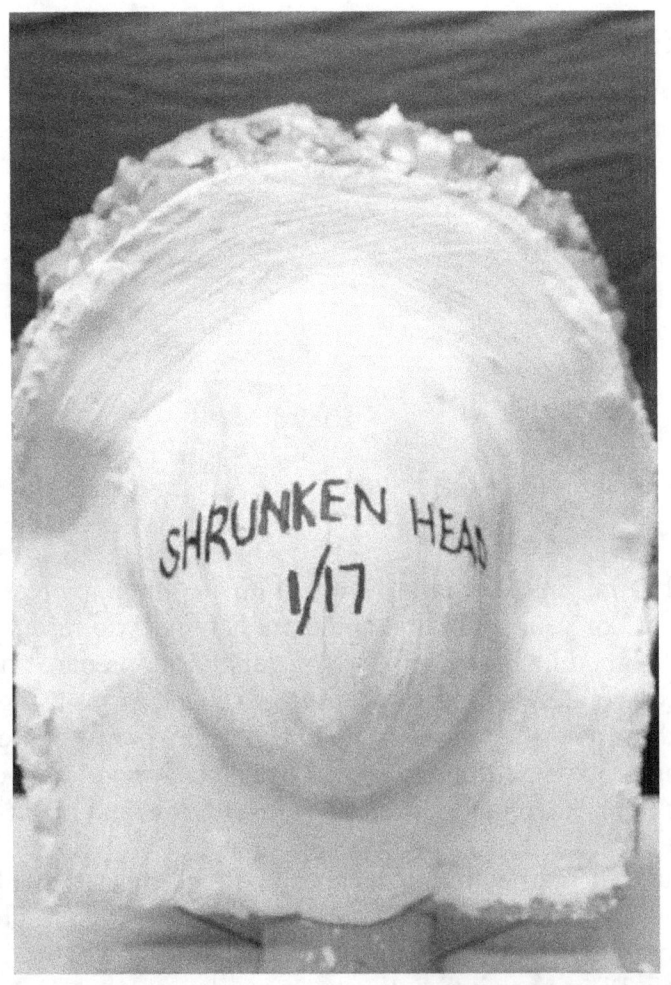

STEP 4: THE MOLD

Congratulations, you have successfully sculpted your shrunken head!

Now it's time to destroy it.

Molding Materials

1. 10 lbs of UltraCal 30 plaster
2. A half yard of burlap cut into 3"x3" squares
3. Petroleum jelly (release agent)
4. A disposable cup for water
5. Latex gloves

Tools

1. Mixing bowl
2. A black marker
3. Chip brushes
4. Dust mask or respirator

I call this the "make or break" step. You are about to create a rigid mold of your sculpture, and there is no way to rescue your work if something goes wrong. None at all. So, prepare yourself. I've been creating shrunken heads, masks, and props using this method for over twenty years, and each time I confront the molding process a little fear creeps over me. A good thing, too, since it helps keep me focused on steps, timing, and material use.

When a craftsman with two decades of experience says "I have a checklist I adhere to while completing this task," you might want to do the same! I have provided a checklist for you at the end of the book. Please use it to help you remember steps you've read here.

> **FUN FACT:** I use a checklist because I have made so many molds that I get complacent. Complacency breeds mistakes. This won't make any sense to you right now, but it will by the time you have finished the book, and certainly by the time you've made a mold. I was making a mold for a mask a few years ago. By that time, I had

made a lot of molds. I was working through the process, or so I thought. I didn't discover the grave mistake I had made until I had poured the latex into the mold. Suddenly there was latex everywhere.

While I was still creating the mold, I flipped the first side over to start the second. I was supposed to remove the clay from the registration marks and leave the clay representing the pry marks (We will talk about all of these this later). Instead, I left both the registrations and pry mark clay in place. The result was huge holes where plaster should have been. When I started pouring latex in the mold, the registration VOIDS were allowing latex to flow out of the vacant space and onto the floor. I couldn't believe the mistake I had made. From that day on, I used a checklist to keep me on the right path.

Time

Timing is critical. You never want to be stuck in a position where time is forcing you to work faster than necessary, so you need to carefully plan your mold. *Never* leave one side of your mold half done. As you are about to learn, there are four layers to each side of a plaster mold. If you have completed two of the four layers, and need to leave your project for the night, DON'T. That's just inviting catastrophe.

Always give yourself enough time to finish all four layers before you leave. Friends and family will understand. If they don't, get new friends and family. Even if you can only do one side of a two-part mold, make sure that one side is 100% completed.

> **NOTE:** Plaster and WED Clay are a lot alike. They both draw moisture from their surroundings. That can sometimes be a problem. A student of mine kept leaving the class to take phone calls. She managed to get the first two layers of plaster onto their mold, but with the constant breaks, her mold was left unfinished. Rather than stay late to catch up, she decided to leave the mold for the next day.
>
> Everyone removed the plastic bags from their molds to continue working the next afternoon. When she removed hers, she made a horrific discovery. The two plaster layers were rather thin. The clay from the sculpture had pulled water from those thin layers, causing it to crack. When it cracked, the plaster started to fall apart. She had to start all over again.

Materials at the Ready

Materials are another issue. Always make sure you have all the materials you need for a mold ready and available. You don't want to start the first layer of a mold and then discover that you don't have enough plaster to start the second, third, or fourth layers. Also, don't skimp. Never make a thinner plaster mix because you don't have enough plaster to mix it correctly. Stretching out materials is never good where molds are concerned.

These things are so important that I'm going to repeat them. Call it The Mantra of Molding:

1. Follow a checklist.
2. Give yourself enough time to finish all four layers.
3. Make sure everything you need is ready and on hand from the start.

PRO TIP: First things first, test your plaster. Mix a small batch of UltraCal 30 up in a mixing cup and let it set. If the plaster sets, then you are good. If it doesn't set in about sixty to seventy minutes, then there may be something wrong with your material. It's better to find out at this stage than to discover there is something wrong after you pour the material onto your sculpture.

Sealing the Sculpture

Most effects artists, me included, use a clear matte spray-paint called Krylon Crystal Clear. I spray two or three coats over the entire sculpture. Follow the directions on the spray can, and allow the spray to completely dry before moving on. Please remember to wear your respirator.

The spray will create a bit of a barrier between the sculpture and the next step. Since the next step can be a bit time-consuming, the spray also protects the WED Clay sculpture from drying out.

Building the Caseline

DEFINITION: A caseline is the dividing wall between the halves of a mold--in this case, the dividing line between the two halves of a 2-piece mold (the front and the back).

You are going to center your sculpted head on a clean flat surface like a table or counter. It might be a good idea to find a scrap piece of plywood to use as a barrier between the table and the mold. This step can get messy.

Please make sure you can walk around the surface on which you are working. You don't need to walk 360 degrees around it, though that would be nice. You should, however, be able to easily access every inch of the area comfortably, making sure there is a clear view of the shrunken head on all sides. You should be able to work around the whole sculpture without causing damage to it, or the work you put into the caseline.

Just as important, make sure it's ok to use that surface. Don't tick off your spouse, parent, or guardian because you thought molding a sculpture on a priceless antique was safe. It would be hilarious for me to hear, but not so good for you. Consider yourself warned.

Take your marker and draw a dividing line on your sculpture like the one illustrated in Diagram 32. This is your guide for the caseline. It represents the two halves of the mold you are building. Take care to draw the line on the outside edge of the ear, but don't draw the dotted line *through* the ear. I will explain why in a moment.

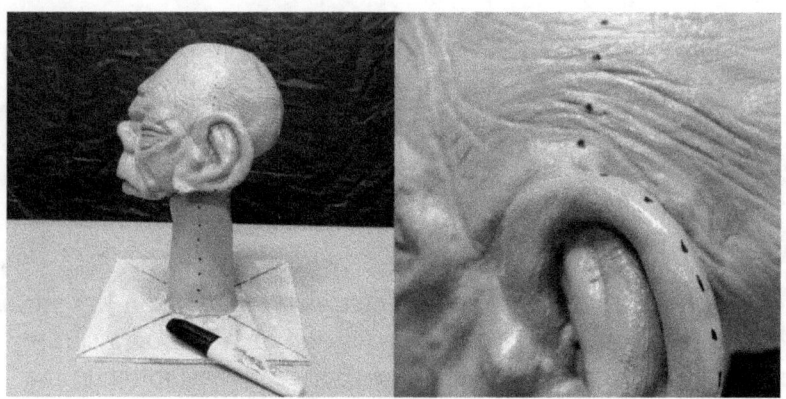

DIAGRAM 32

Mark a spot on the plywood and place small balls of clay on it. Then cover that clay with some plastic wrap or an old plastic shopping bag. Lay your project face up on the platform, with the back of your sculpture's head resting on the plastic bag and the balls of clay. The clay and plastic work like a pillow, preventing your sculpt from being dented. The plastic keeps the clay balls from sticking to your sculpture. Also, use enough clay to ensure the sculpture is level, or as level as you can get it.

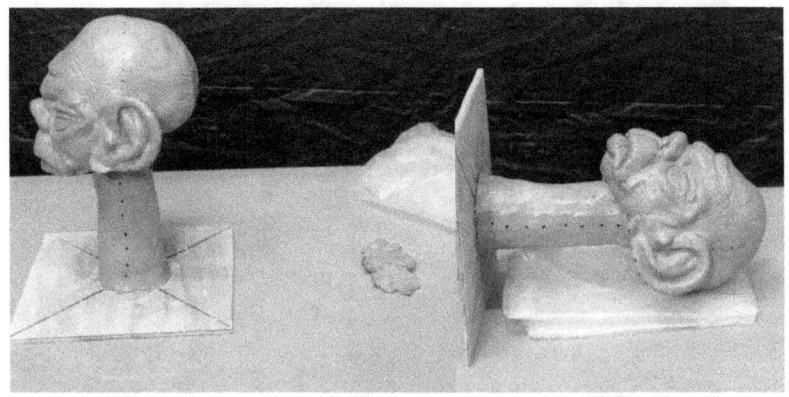

DIAGRAM 33

Now, you need to build a mound of clay up to the dotted line you just drew. Build up your clay mound on both sides of the sculpture, but not past it. You can use clay alone, or a combination of wood and clay together if you want to save on clay. Scrap pieces of 2x4 boards are great for this, and cost next to nothing—especially if they were just lying around in the first place.

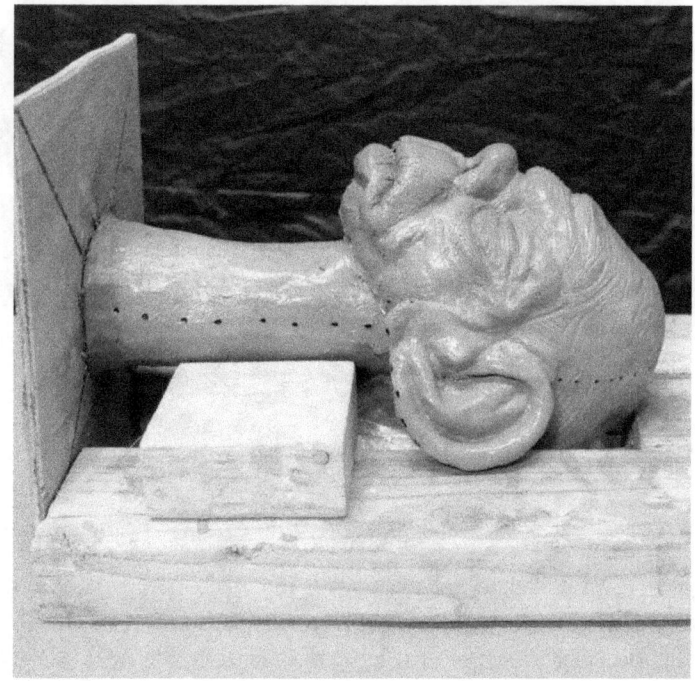

DIAGRAM 34

I suggest using a hot-glue gun to glue your 2x4s to the surface of that plywood barrier you placed between the sculpture and table. If you don't have a hot-glue gun get one. There are alternatives but they aren't the best. You can use wood glue. It takes much, much longer to set but will hold in place. Getting it apart later is going to suck, though. You can also use super glue or caulking, but my suggestion is to spend the $5 on a cheap hot-glue gun: it's absolutely worth it. You don't want things moving around when you build the first layer of a caseline.

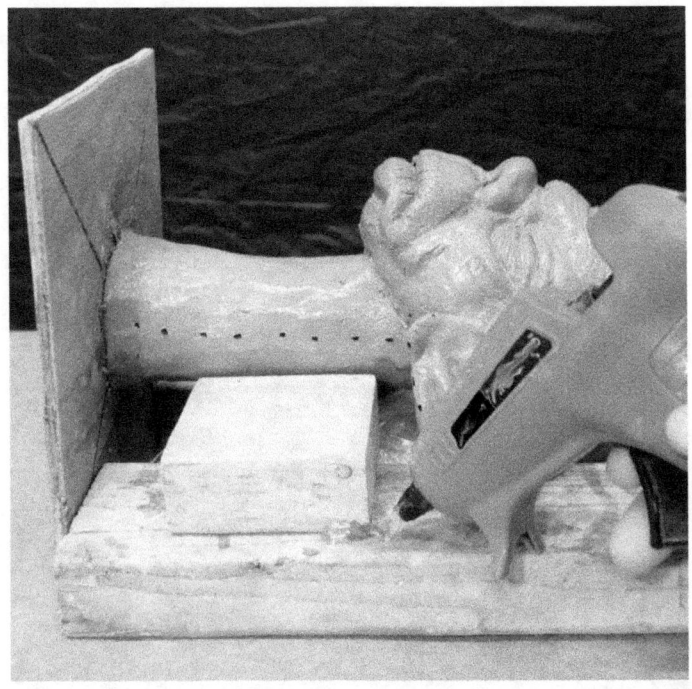

DIAGRAM 35

Whatever you do, don't nick or dent your sculpture! Get the wood and clay of the caseline close to it, but not too close. We will get closer with the clay in a bit, but not right now.

Notice how the dotted line in Diagram 36 doesn't cross the ear? This means that one side of the mold (the front half) will contain the front of the ear, while the other side of the mold (the back half) will contain the back of the ear. To achieve this, we will only build up to the dotted line on the ear, on the neck, and on the top of the head, just as shown in Diagram 36. The area around the ear is like a ditch, and it will double as a registration later.

DEFINITION: A mold registration is a point or shape that forces a mold to fit together only one way—the right way. Registrations also keep the mold from sliding on the caseline. If two halves of a mold slide out of place during the casting process, then liquid latex would spill out, ruining your cast as well as wasting material.

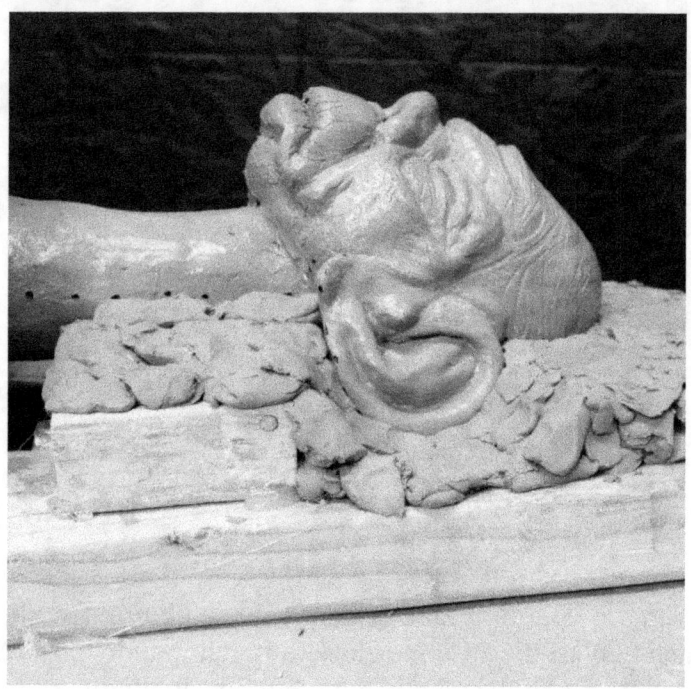

DIAGRAM 36

The area illustrated in Diagram 36 represents the clay level you will need to create. After the buildup, this surface should be smooth and must be flush with the sculpture. Do your best to insure your clay level is at a strong right angle from the sculpture. This is very important. If you create an unlevel wall, the area where the two mold halves connect will be weak and could break off, damaging your final piece.

Pay close attention to the ear in Diagram 36. Notice how the clay wall contours the ear? You want to ensure that the area around the ear is wider at the top of the ditch and more narrow at the bottom. If this was reversed for some reason, you would be in serious trouble when you tried to separate the two mold halves. We call this an undercut, and it is the kiss of death for a mold.

Undercuts

DEFINITION: An undercut is an area where the plaster surface of one mold half is locked on to the other, which almost always results in a broken mold. Image a cue ball. The ball has an equator—the point where the ball is split into two perfect hemispheres. Now imagine that you have pressed the cue ball into wet plaster, right up to its equator. When the plaster cures, you should be able to remove the cue ball without damaging the plaster. But if you pushed the cue ball *past* the equator, even a little bit, then the plaster would have the cue ball in its grasp with no easy release. The only way to retrieve the cue ball in that situation would be to break the cement (your mold in real life), break the cue ball (your sculpture in real life), or both. More times than not, an undercut is going to break both.

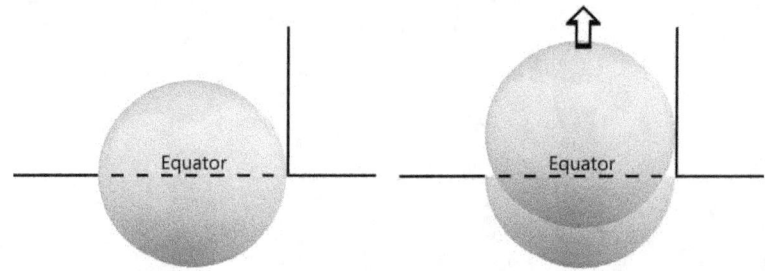

DIAGRAM 37 A

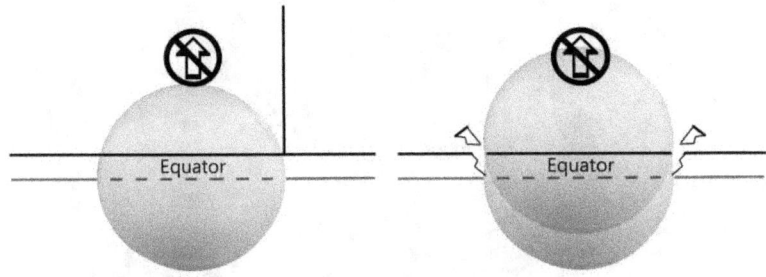

DIAGRAM 37 B

Once we have built the clay level up to the dotted line, we can start closing the gap between the caseline and the sculpture as seen in Diagram 38. Make sure the clay surface of your caseline is as smooth as possible, and meets the side of your sculpture seamlessly. Make sure there are no divots or holes around the sculpture/caseline border. Once you have made this line as smooth as glass, you can move onto the next step.

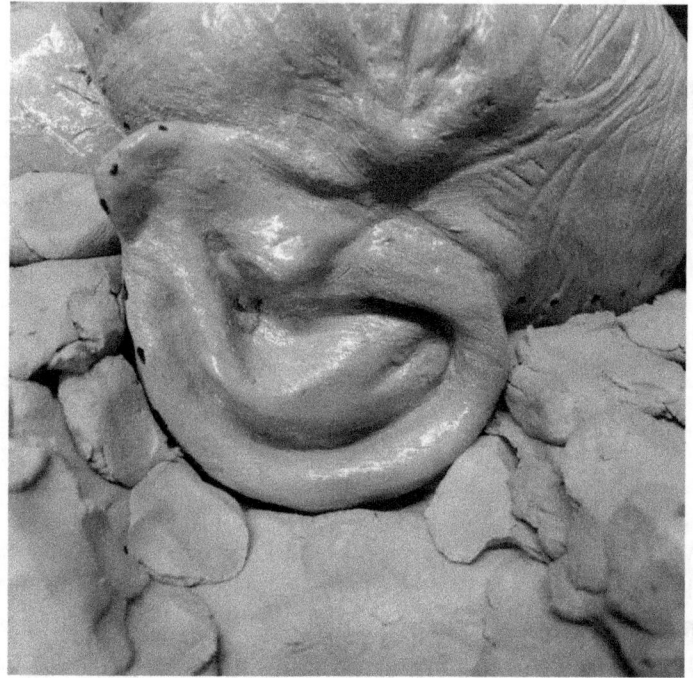

DIAGRAM 38

We are going to talk about building a clay wall in just a moment, but before we can move on to that task, we must first smooth the caseline that is shown in Diagram 38. All the balls of clay should be smoothed out. This is where the clay will actually come into contact with the sculpture. We do it this way so there is a minimum amount of clay debris that can potentially become stuck to the sculpture.

When you are done smoothing your caseline it should look like mine in Diagram 39.

Shrunken Heads

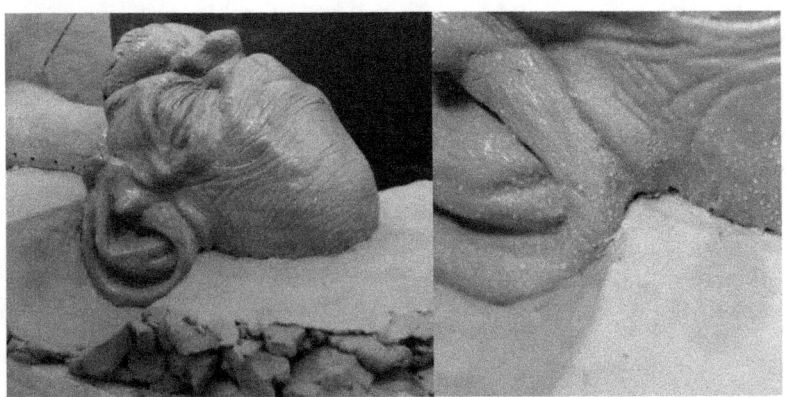

DIAGRAM 39

Build the Retaining Wall

Now we need to build a clay retaining wall around our sculpture. I show this in Diagram 40. One thing I'll point out is that your walls should be at least a quarter inch thick and about an inch to an inch and a half tall. This will withstand the weight of the liquid plaster when it gets added later.

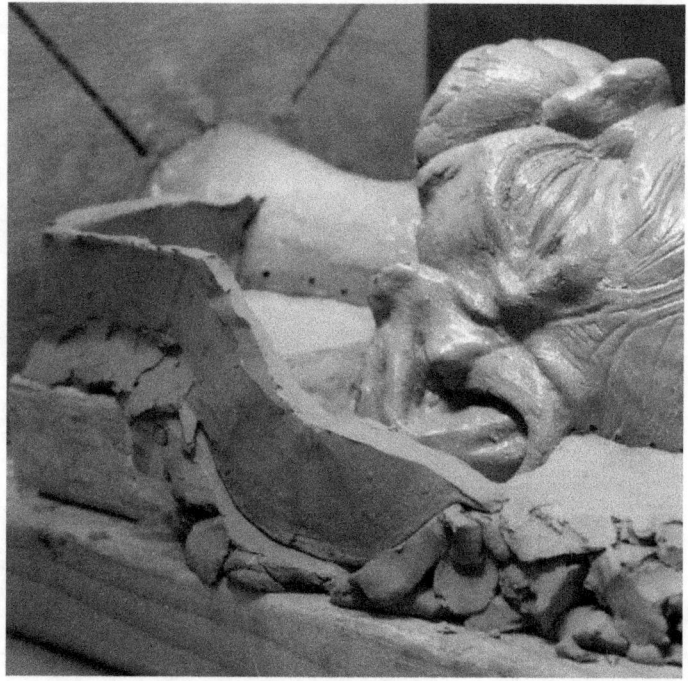

DIAGRAM 40

Your wall doesn't need to be very high. In general practice, the walls I build for molds are about as high as a yard stick is thick. Maybe the width plus half. You want it high enough to trap liquid plaster and to make a nice thick plaster caseline, but short enough so you don't end up using more plaster than your mold needs.

The next step is to make this wall watertight. We do that by smearing the clay at the base of the wall into the clay of the caseline you just built. We are only smearing the outside base of the wall, not the inside. Leave the inside of the wall alone. You can use a popsicle stick or sculpting tool to smear the clay.

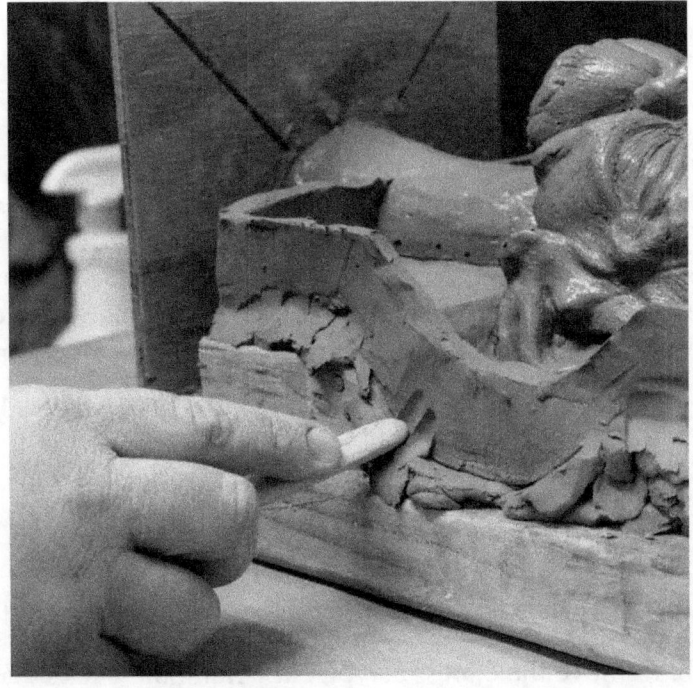

DIAGRAM 41

Registration

As I stated earlier, registrations (sometimes referred to as keys) are points on the mold that force the mold to fit together one way—the right way. Once we have the wall constructed, we can create the registrations for side one of our mold.

This is how I make my registrations. I roll out a small slab of WED Clay on a flat surface. The slab should be about a fourth of an inch thick and a few inches square. I am not going to use the whole piece, but I need enough to cut out my shape. My registration is somewhere in the middle.

I am going to use a loop tool to cut out my shape. You might be thinking a knife or a spatula tool would be best—and it might be. I like the loop tool because there is less surface space on the tool itself. The surface on a blade-like tool tends to collect moisture and debris from the WED Clay, which makes the second cut a lot rougher and often warps the line on the registration. Sure, you can clean off the blade between cuts, but why? With the loop tool, I don't have to.

Mold making can be a pain in the butt. There are a lot of steps and processes to pay attention to. This is one way to lessen the desire to throw your sculpture through the window.

Using my loop tool, I make a forty-five-degree cut along one side of the slab. I will repeat this cut on the top and bottom edges of the slab. Remove the excess as you cut. Along the back edge, the edge opposite of the long forty-five-degree cut we initially made, I will make a ninety-degree cut. Nice and flat. This is the edge that will rest against the clay wall.

Diagram 42 below will show you the process I just described. The result is a clean and well-made registration that we will place in key points of our caseline.

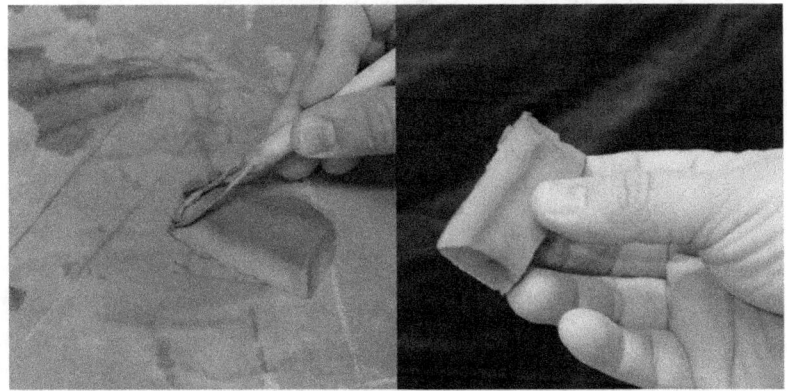

DIAGRAM 42

The next step is to place the registration on the caseline. That canal around each ear will work as a larger registration. I will use one of these geometric shapes I've just created and place it at the top of the head.

Even if your creature is asymmetrical, where the mold is concerned you want to get into the habit of thinking of your mold as a mirror image. What you do to one side, you should also do to the other. For instance, when you are placing registrations and pry marks, you really want them to mirror each other in terms of placement. If you have a pry mark or registration placed by the forehead of one side, you want to place another in the exact same spot on the other side.

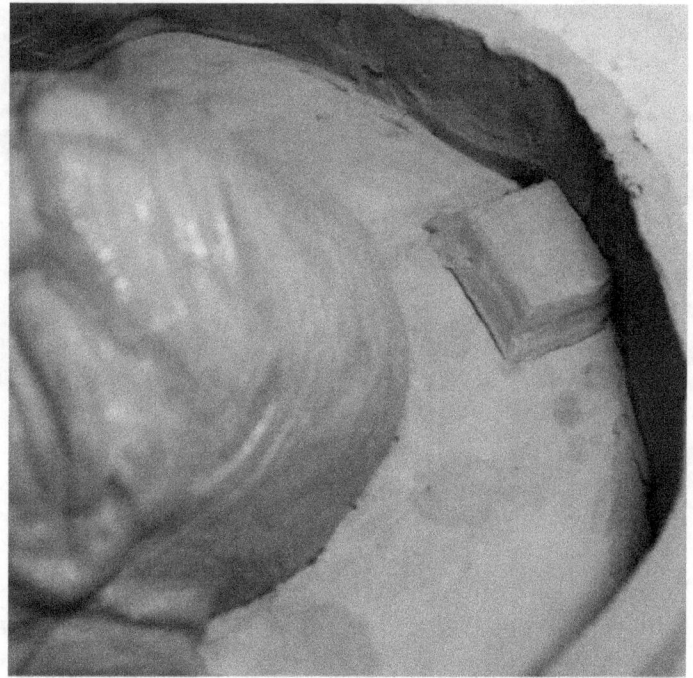

DIAGRAM 43

I just mentioned pry marks a couple times. For the sake of this tutorial, I am saving those for later. We will discuss those during the build process for side two of our two-piece mold.

Once you have placed your registration like I have, you can move on to the next step.

Sealing

I suggest sealing this project with Krylon Crystal Clear spray. I use the matte finish because it seems to keep the liquid plaster from beading up on the surface of the sculpture better than gloss does. It's still going to bead up, just not as badly. Gloss spray seems to act like car wax. Ever see water bead up on a freshly wax car? This happens to plaster when you use gloss.

I have seen other artists use gloss spray, then a dulling agent afterward to keep the plaster from beading up on the surface of the sculpture. Why not just buy the matte finish and save a step? Again, it's one of those stress-relieving things I talked about earlier.

If all you have is gloss spray, and you can't afford to pick up a can of matte spray now, you can use the gloss. Eventually, through the process of applying the plaster to the surface you will be able to overcome the beading issue, but it's a pain in the butt. So, if it's all you have, use it.

Two coats of either spray, all around the caseline, should be fine. Always wait for the spray to dry between coats, and before moving on to the next step.

PLASTER LAYER 1: The First Splash Coat

Mix a *small* batch of UltraCal 30 plaster following the instructions on the bag. MAKE SURE YOU ARE WEARING LATEX GLOVES AND SOME SORT OF RESPIRATOR. UltraCal 30 is the most commonly used plaster for making molds that produce latex casts, because of its superior qualities. Never use plaster of Paris to make your molds. It's a bad material for this application. You will need at least ten pounds of plaster to make this mold. More than likely you won't use it all, but having extra on hand just in case is a good practice. Especially if you make a mistake with a batch and it kicks too fast.

The first and second layers of your mold are commonly referred to as the SPLASH COATS. These are thin layers that capture all the detail of the sculpture. One problem with splash coats is that they can retain air bubbles, which will need to be worked out of the plaster.

> **NOTE:** Air bubbles are about to become your arch enemy—at least while you are molding and casting. Find these enemies and destroy them! Kill them! Kill them all!

Another problem is that these layers are so thin that as they cure they can easily collapse or shatter if left for a long period. As I mentioned earlier, your sculpture is made of WED Clay. WED is trying to leach water from the plaster and the plaster is trying to leach water from the WED. If it happens too quickly the plaster will crack. Once you start a mold you really do have to see it through.

While I highly suggest *you* follow the instructions on the UltraCal 30 container, I actually have a visual process I adhere to, which has served me very well over the years. My mixing process is as follows: start by adding about half an inch of water to a large mixing container. I use a two-and-a-half-quart container from Home Depot. They cost about ninety-nine cents and are good for multiple molds before they finally give up the ghost. So, as you follow along, understand that I will be using this contain to reference what I am doing.

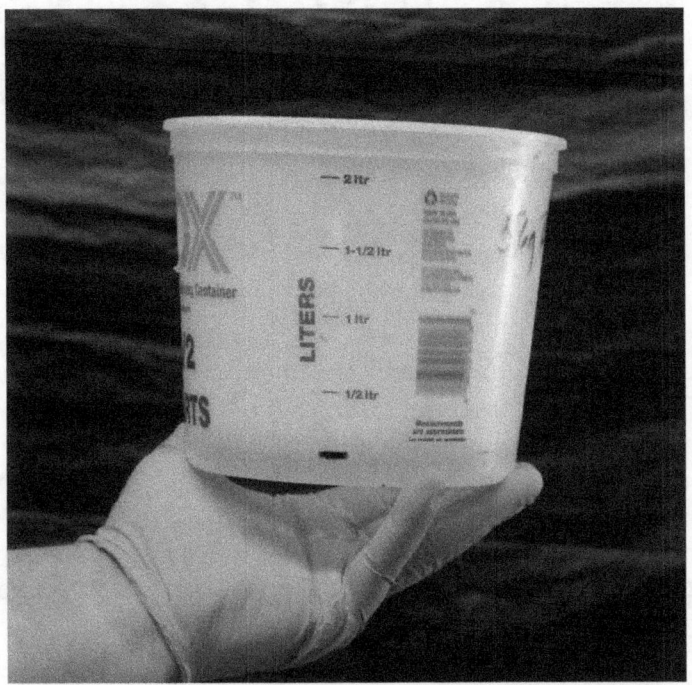

DIAGRAM 44

Next, scoop out some plaster, making absolutely sure you don't introduce any water into the bag of plaster. I find it best to sift the plaster out of my scoop and into the water of the mixing container. This allows the plaster to absorb the water in little amounts and reduces clumps. If you want, you can use a mixing stick, electric mixer, or drill to blend the material. I typically use my gloved hand.

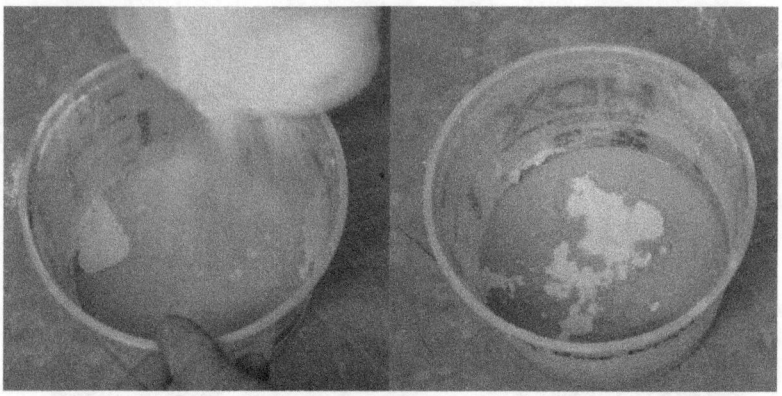

DIAGRAM 45

As you mix, make sure to break up any clumps of plaster that form. You want the final mix to have the look and smooth consistency of a thick milkshake. I hope I don't need to say this, but don't drink it. I wouldn't even bother if I hadn't had someone do it once before. Seriously.

Once the plaster is mixed you are at the moment of truth, because after you pour it onto the sculpture there is no turning back.

I start by holding the mixing container over the sculpture and reach in for a handful of plaster, which I lightly drizzle onto the sculpture. Once the sculpture is thinly coated, I use a chip brush to pull the plaster around the surface, pressing it gently into all the wrinkles, folds, cracks, and crevices. If you don't do this you will have air bubbles in the mold, which will lead to a poorly finished product, or a weak mold.

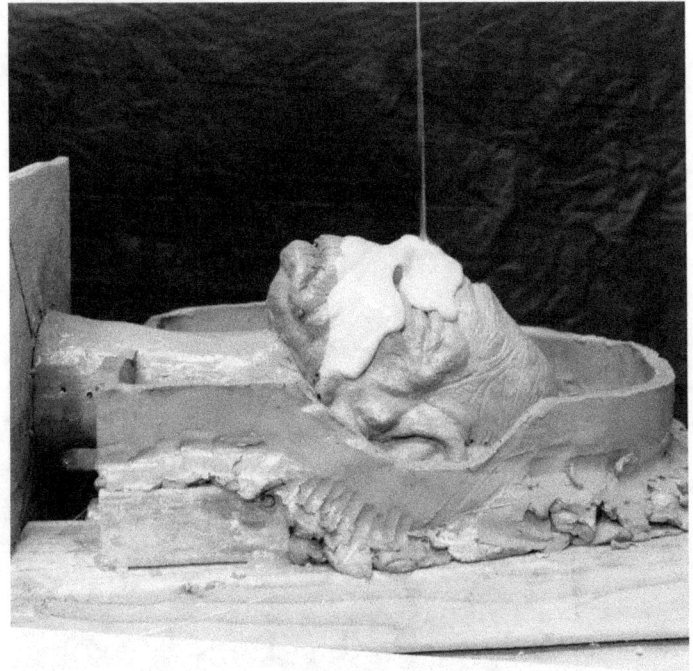

DIAGRAM 46

Pay close attention to the border where the caseline and sculpture meet —you don't want air bubbles there either. These corner spaces are notorious for collecting bubbles.

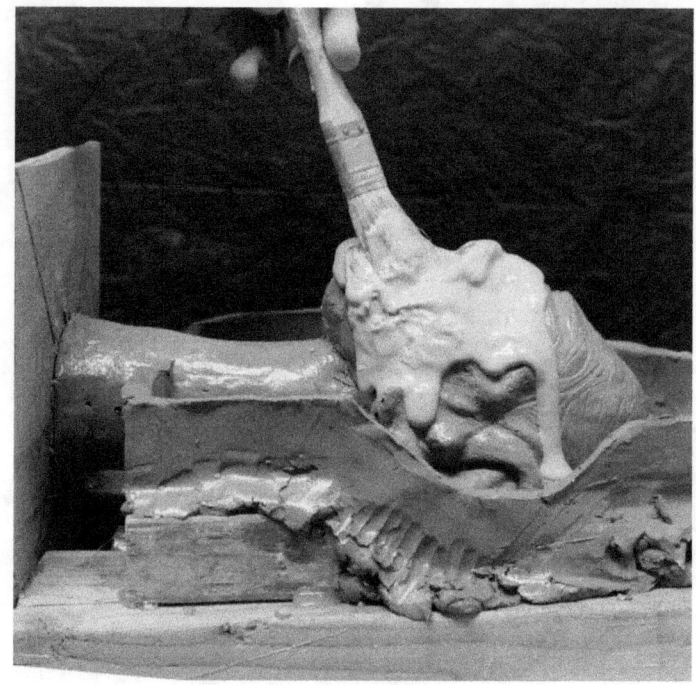

DIAGRAM 47

Keep this up until you have exhausted what you mixed in the container. There's an important rule of thumb here: *if you mix it, use it*. Hardened plaster in a mixing bucket is a pain to pull out, and a complete waste of materials that could have been used in the mold. Therefore, you should never mix larger batches than you actually need.

Once the entire sculpture has been coated, let the material set for twenty to sixty minutes, and then repeat. Try to leave this layer alone to cure. If you work it too long with the chip brush you will start to remove plaster from the surface of the sculpture. You don't want to do that, since it defeats the purpose.

I suggest leaving the layer for about twenty to sixty minutes. This is an estimate that comes with some environmental factors. Humidity and temperature have a huge impact on cure time. A seventy to eighty-degree dry room yields the best results. Of course, plaster will still cure in cooler temperatures and even under water. The more humid and cool the environment, the longer it will take to cure, so waiting for the plaster to kick (cure) is very much like watching paint dry or waiting for water to boil. Hope you have a good book—perhaps *Latex Mask Making* or *Creature Fur and Hair*, two great *Workshops with Russ Adams*.

Heh heh heh!

> **PRO TIP:** I call this a "Pro Tip" but really it should be a "Ebenezer Scrooge Tip." As a business owner I am always looking for ways to save money. The cost of consumables, materials that you only get one or two uses out of, can really add up across the board.
>
> Early on, when I was just struggling to keep the studio doors open, I would do things like extend the use of my chip brushes. Basically, this meant taking the time to wash them out between uses. You have four layers to each side of a plaster mold. We were using a different brush per layer. Multiply that by the number of sides, three to four side molds in some cases, and the cost of these brushes started to become noticeable. Do the math. That's twelve to sixteen brushes per mold. At seventy-five cents a brush, we were adding nearly twelve dollars to the cost of each mold for brushes alone. We make a lot of molds, so that calculated to a metric-butt-ton of money and waste material. Don't even get me started on some of the other stuff.
>
> So, if you could spend seventy-five cents instead of twelve dollars, wouldn't you? Wash out your brushes. Have a cup of water on hand to get them good and

cleaned out between layers. AND DON'T LEAVE THE BRUSH IN THE CUP OF WATER! I just told you plaster cures underwater. If you leave that brush in the cup, the plaster sediment will set up around your bristles and you just wasted a brush.

Also, don't rinse your brush or containers in the sink. The plaster will set up in your pipes. Keep all plaster away from all sinks. I always have a five-gallon pail full of water nearby to rinse things off. You should do the same.

PLASTER LAYER 2: The Second Splash Coat

Spritz a little water on the surface of the hardened plaster just before applying the next layer. Don't go crazy with it. Just a couple spritzes will work. This is really a repeat of the last step. One thing to keep in mind, though—each layer you apply is going to cure a little faster than the last, because the previous layer is leaching water from the one you are adding, creating— you guessed it— air bubbles. Air bubbles are really the enemy in mold making and casting in latex. As I have said, and will keep saying, you want to avoid air bubbles because they weaken a mold, and can mess with the outcome of a cast…esthetically speaking.

Oh! Wash out your brush.

Once the second splash coat is cured, you should immediately move on to the next step.

PLASTER LAYER 3: The Insurance Layer

I call this the insurance layer because it's how you insure that a cracked mold isn't a lost mold.

Once again, start by spritzing the surface of the previous layer with a little water. I am going to mix this plaster exactly as I did for the last two splash coat layers. I like to lay a thin layer of plaster over the previous layers to reduce the risk of trapped air. I drizzle some plaster on the previous cured layer and coat it with the chip brush.

The difference between this layer the others is burlap. I have a good pile of pre-cut burlap squares handy. They are about three inches by three inches, a perfect size for this application. Anything smaller starts to unravel and causes a mess. Larger squares tend to bunch up rather than lie flat, which becomes an air-bubble trap.

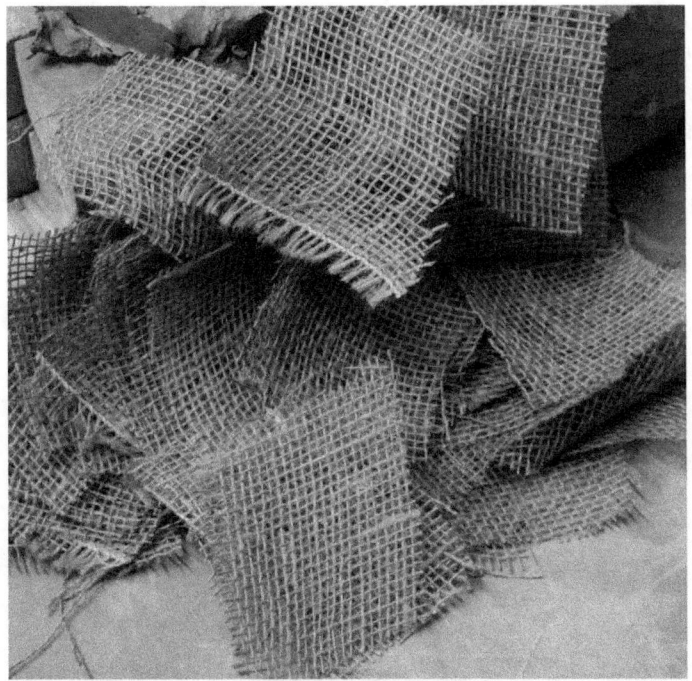

DIAGRAM 48

PRO TIP: Get your burlap at Home Depot's garden section, not a fabric store (unless there is a major sale). Once something is listed for sale as a crafty item, the powers-that-be hike up the price. I recently found a yard stick with a hefty seven-dollar price tag at a very well-known fabric chain. The same wooden stick was under a dollar at Home Depot. How much do you think this fabric giant hikes up the price of that burlap? We don't need neon colored burlap either, plan brown potato-sack-looking burlap is fine.

Then dunk the burlap squares into the plaster mix *one at a time*. Trying to coat multiple squares just makes a mess. Squeegee off any excess plaster from the square with your fingers, then lay it down nearest to the clay retaining wall. Repeat this square by square, working your way from the caseline, then up the sculpture as shown in Diagram 49.

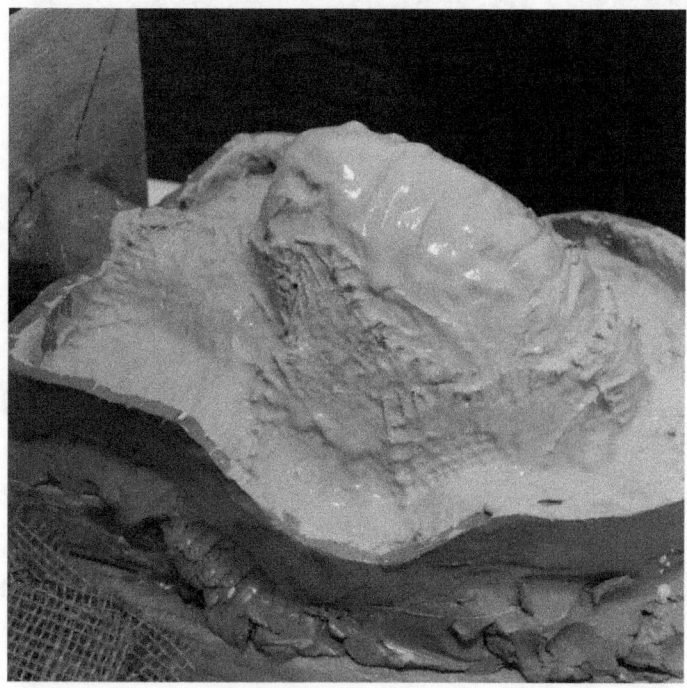

DIAGRAM 49

I like to lay the burlap along the entire caseline first, then lay the next batch slightly above it, making sure to overlap each burlap square a tiny bit. I start here because it's my routine and once I have a pile of burlap on the sculpture it is easy to lose track of what is covered by burlap and what isn't. Having a tried and true method keeps me from wondering if I did or didn't cover something.

Our ever-present risk of air bubbles is worse in this layer, because air can get trapped between new burlap pieces as they are laid down. I use a chip brush to push the burlap into place and squeeze out the air. When you are doing this, be careful that you don't press too hard or you might crack the splash coat layers below.

When the mold is completely covered, the fibers in this layer will hold the mold together if it ever cracks. If it happens to you, it will give you time to get a few more casts out of a dying mold, or to repair the mold in an effort to preserve it.

Remember: a mold is the only thing you have left of your original sculpture. Once that mold is gone, so is that piece. That makes it important to protect your mold from damage or loss.

Once we reach the top of the mold surface with the burlap we can rest, and wait for it to cure before moving on to the next step. I often use my chip brush to comb the surface down and smooth this layer the best I can. Those little fibers can be a pill. You can do another burlap layer if you like, but it's not necessary. One will do the job.

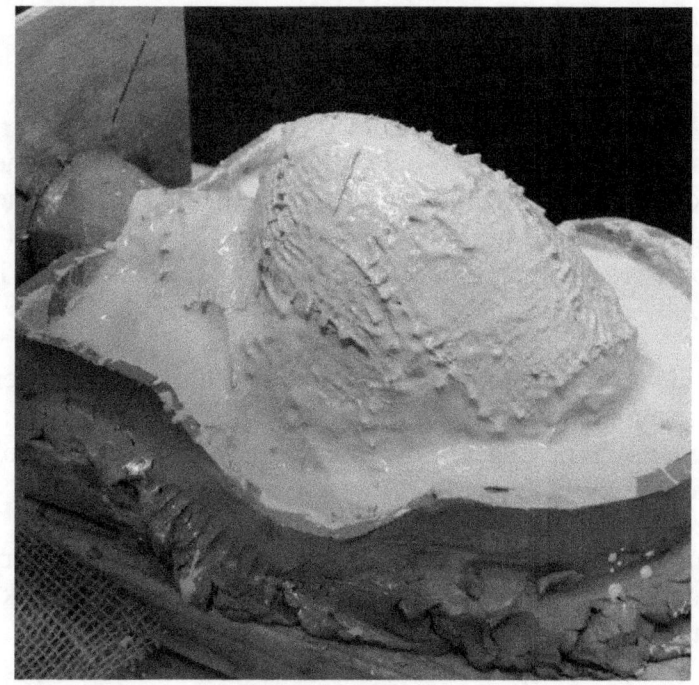

DIAGRAM 50

PLASTER LAYER 4: The Protective Layer

The protective layer is the thickest layer. When I mix plaster for this layer I like it to be the consistency of playdough, which means using less water and more plaster.

When I put this thicker plaster on, I am scooping it out of the pail with a gloved hand and spreading it around the surface of the mold. A lot of artists use a kidney shaped tool to shape and smooth this layer, but I just use a chip brush. The brush still shapes the plaster into a smooth clean surface, but the bristles leave a texture behind that allows me to get a better grip on bigger molds.

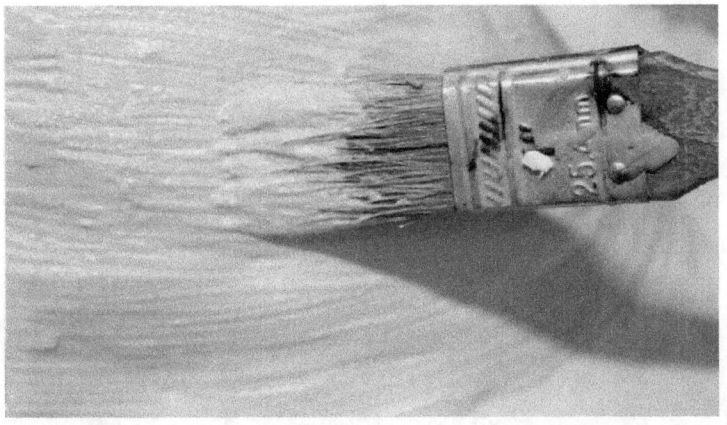

DIAGRAM 51

When you are done, the shell should look a lot like Diagram 52. You should strive to make the surface as clean as possible. When plaster cures, a rough or choppy surface can cause injuries.

Plaster edges can be sharp. Also, those rough areas can start to chip and break away, weakening your mold.

Congrats! You have finished the first half of your mold. Let's celebrate! After the mold cures, grab a marker and write the name of the project on the mold along with the date. It's kind of a milestone…a half-way point tradition in my shop.

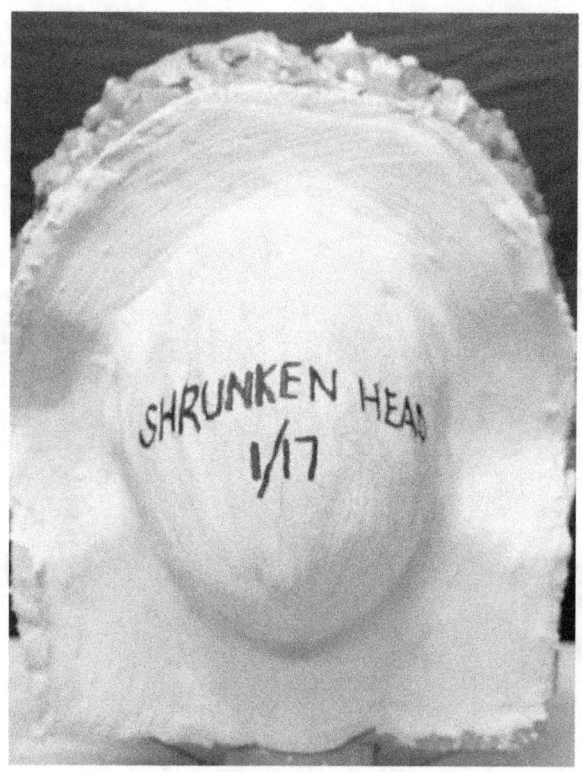

DIAGRAM 52

Prepping for Side Two

Once the final layer in the first half of your mold has hardened for 20-60 minutes, you can prepare to make the second half of the mold. This is the only time it would be considered okay for you to leave your mold and come back the next day. If you do this make sure you cover the mold project with a sheet of plastic.

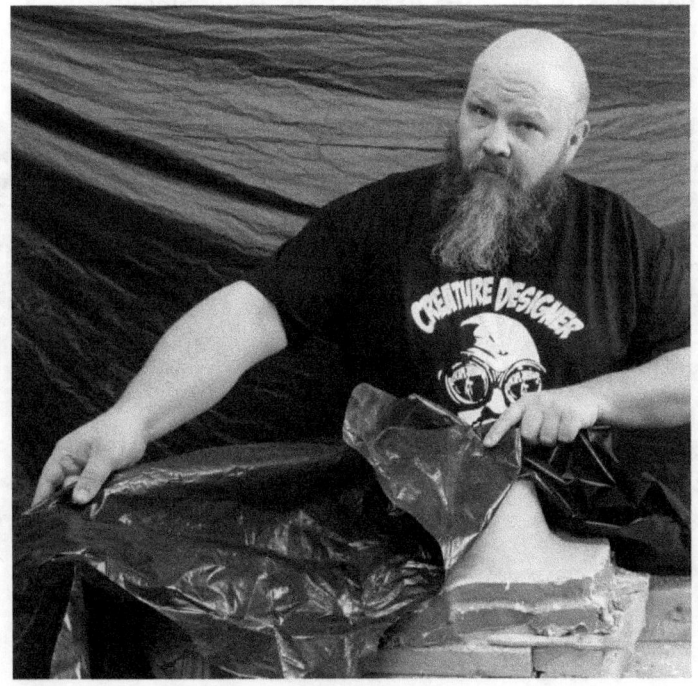

DIAGRAM 53

When you are ready to move on, you can. Begin by slowly removing some of the surrounding clay from the caseline.

If you used a hot glue gun to glue the 2x4s to the plywood under the sculpture, good news: we can break that bond pretty easily. Just pour rubbing alcohol onto the hot-glue seam. That will weaken the glue's hold on the plywood and 2x4s, letting you pop them apart. If you used wood glue or caulking, it's going to be harder. You may need to pry it up.

We are going to turn the entire piece upside down on a flat, level surface. It may roll a bit, so we will use the 2x4s we just liberated from side one to stabilize the mold. You can also use clay in combination with the 2x4s to make the mold stable.

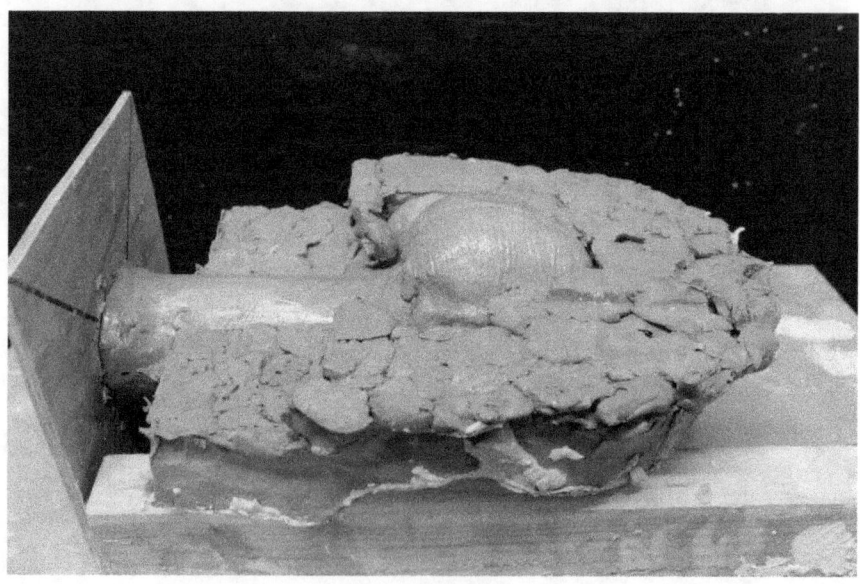

DIAGRAM 54

Once the mold is secure we will start removing the excess clay. The goal is to pull the clay away from the plaster without damaging your sculpture. So be careful! You will need to be particularly careful not to damage your work. If the surface gets nicked, it can be easily fixed in most cases. Getting the detail to match up can be tricky if it carried over to the front and it's now incased in plaster. With this character, it might not be an issue and could play to the dynamic. On the other hand, if you wanted it there you would have put it there in the first place. Just go slow, and remove the clay methodically.

We will be removing the registration clay as well. You don't want to repeat my mistake. Do you recall my story about leaving the registration clay in place? This is the reason why I have a checklist on me each time I mold. Get those suckers out of there.

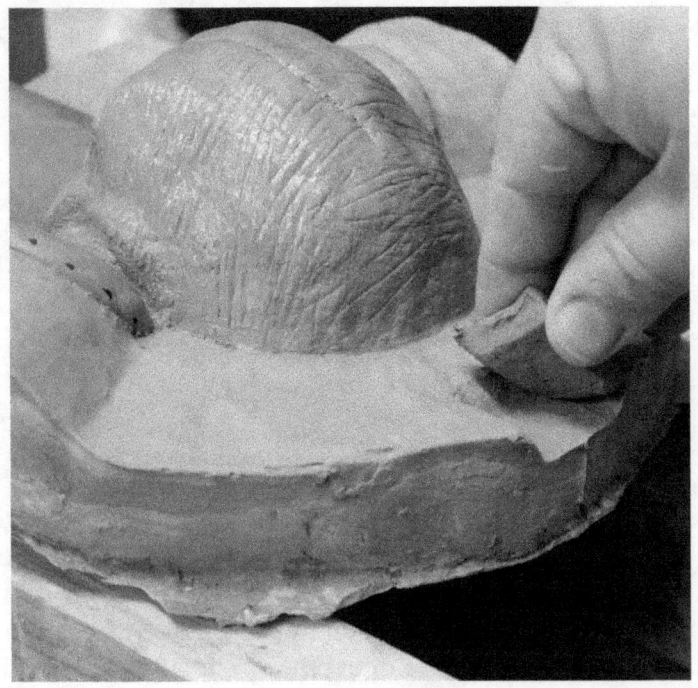

DIAGRAM 55

During the cleanup, you might encounter a few small problems. One of these is the nicks we talked about a moment ago. Another problem you are likely to have will be the area around the head where the clay from the caseline came in direct contact with the clay of the sculpture. This is going to take some time to clean up. More than likely we are going to be doing some touch-up sculpting. It's ok. It happens, but this is where those photographs you took will be helpful. The photos will be helpful in matching or recreating any detail that might have been obliterated.

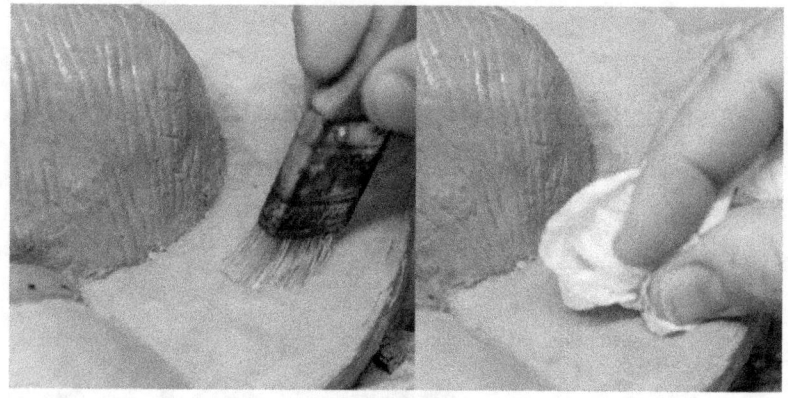

DIAGRAM 56

Once you have removed the buildup, make sure the plaster surface of the caseline is clean. This is important but delicate work, so take your time. Use the spray bottle and some paper towels to help. You can also use a chip brush to get this surface spotlessly clean. Any debris left on the caseline will keep the two halves of the mold from fitting together perfectly. This can result in leaks, heavy flashing (which we will discuss in later sections of this book), and material waste.

Here is the other problem you might encounter during the cleanup stage. The big issue with cleanup is water. We need the water to break down the clay remnants on the caseline, but in doing so it could easily break down the detail of your sculpture. So, make sure you are being conservative with the water bottle. Chase the excess water with some paper towels.

Once you have cleaned the surface of the caseline, dry it off and coat it with petroleum jelly. Plaster will lock to plaster, so you need a mold release to allow them to separate with ease. Petroleum jelly is, in my opinion, the best material for the job.

I apply it with a 1" chip brush for the broad areas, and a smaller paint brush to get all the areas closest to the sculpture—the border where the caseline and sculpture meet, around the sculpture's ears, etc. Set the petroleum jelly aside and make sure you are only using it for mold making.

> **PRO TIP:** I may or may not have changed the gender of the persons involved to protect their identity in the anecdote. Each time I teach the Latex Mask Class at my studio, Escape Design FX, I give a safety briefing. Each time I give it, the speech gets a little longer. That's because during each class someone manages to do something which I could never have imagined. That blunder gets added to the speech for the next class. One of the craziest additions has become the most famous. I begin by telling everyone, "This is a working special-effects studio. Nothing here is what it seems. That said, please don't put anything you find in your mouth."
>
> Why do I say this? We have tub of petroleum jelly in the shop which is clearly mark with a label "shop use molds only." If that wasn't an indicator that this material shouldn't be used for conventional purchases, then the disgusting mashup of debris in the petroleum jelly should have been.

A grown woman, *supervising* her teenage daughter who was taking the class, managed to scoop out a fingerful of this filthy mess and rub it all over her lips—her lips were apparently chapped. It wasn't until the tingling and burning that she became alarmed. From that time on, I have asked that no one put anything they might see into their mouths. Label your petroleum jelly container, and don't use it for anything else.

All steps in mold making are important. Each builds upon the success of the last. If you don't coat the caseline *completely*, even in registration pocket, the two halves will lock together, which will cost you the sculpture and the mold. So be diligent. But at the same time, you want a *thin* coat. Globs of petroleum jelly will replace areas where there should be plaster. So, the thinner the better. Don't coat your sculpture with petroleum jelly, just the plaster. If you thought the plaster beading up on the glossy clear acrylic spray was bad, petroleum jelly on your sculpture takes it to a whole new level.

It's time to reconstruct the clay wall. Refer to Diagram 40 and Diagram 41 to refresh your memory. This time, however, you will want to build the wall a little taller to compensate for sticking it to the side of the plaster. I have provided an example in Diagram 57.

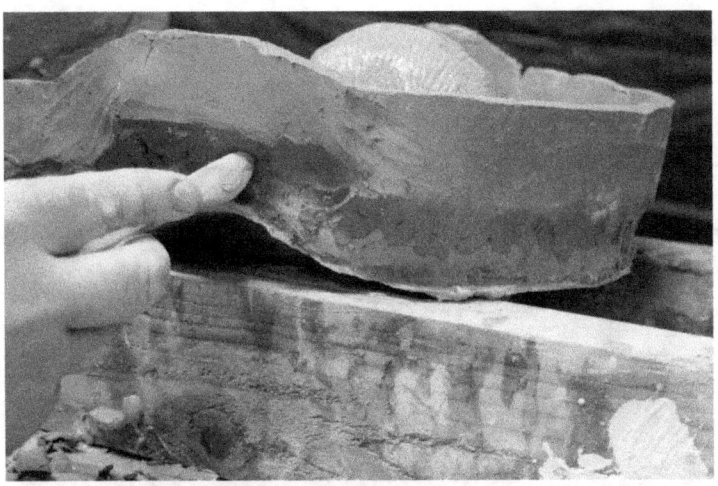

DIAGRAM 57

The first wall was about an inch and a half tall, and about a quarter inch thick. This wall needs to be a bit taller because we aren't stacking it on top of a clay caseline. The caseline is plaster now. We have to stick the wall to the side of that caseline, not on top. The simple reason is this, the wall is a quarter inch thick. Stacking this wall on the plaster means the second half of the mold would be a quarter inch smaller than the other. So, to avoid this, and ensure our molds are flush with each other, we place this clay wall on the side of the plaster.

Pry Marks

Next you need to create a couple of pry marks. These will eventually be small rectangular channels where a small pry bar will slide into and gently force the mold open. Roll out a piece of clay. If you have a small pry bar handy, the clay should only be slightly wider than the pry bar, and just as thick. This is shown in Diagram 58.

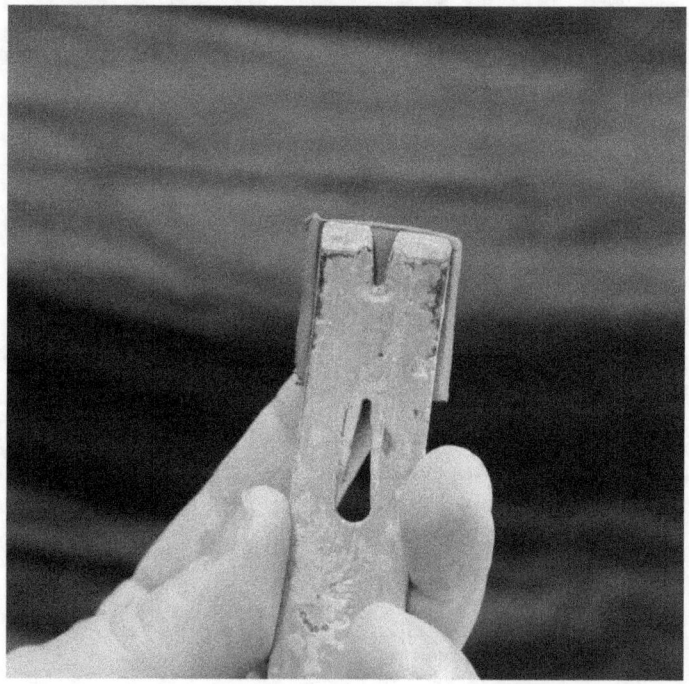

DIAGRAM 58

When the pry bar is forced into this channel we need the fit to be tight. Too much movement and the pry bar isn't going to be as effective when we force the two mold halves apart. I will explain why in more detail when we get to demolding the sculpture.

Diagram 59 shows you where to place theses clay squares. Don't place them near the center of the ear, because this area is curved and your pry bar likely isn't. It's not likely the pry bar would fit when you pry the mold halves apart. You also want to make sure that one side of the square is flush with the inner side of the wall, just like you did with the registrations. These will actually become empty space in the mold later, so you don't want it too close to the sculpture. Make that mistake and during the pouring step, liquid latex will leak out and make a huge mess. Just like it did to me in that Checklist story from earlier.

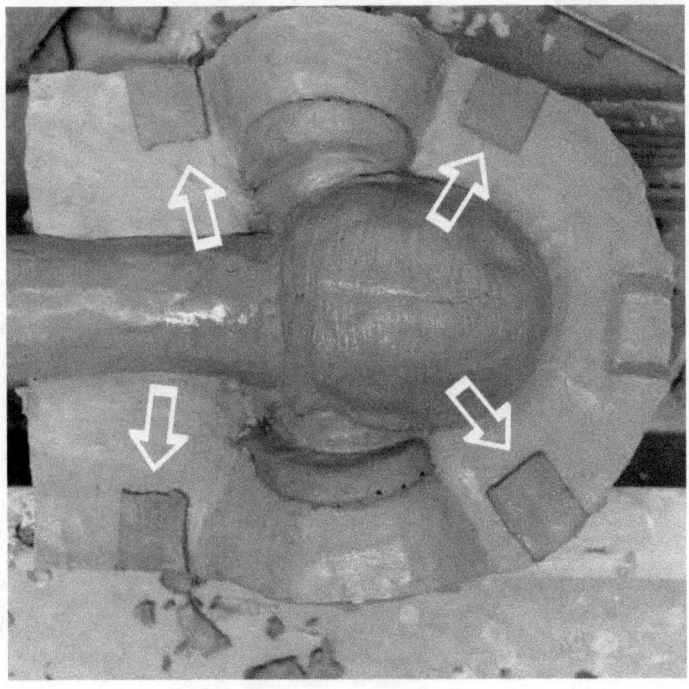

DIAGRAM 59

I like to put two parallel lines on the inside of the clay wall just above the pry marks. These lines indicate where the pry marks are. I do this because the clay can sometimes blend in with the damp plaster. This makes it difficult to find the pry marks when you demold the sculpture.

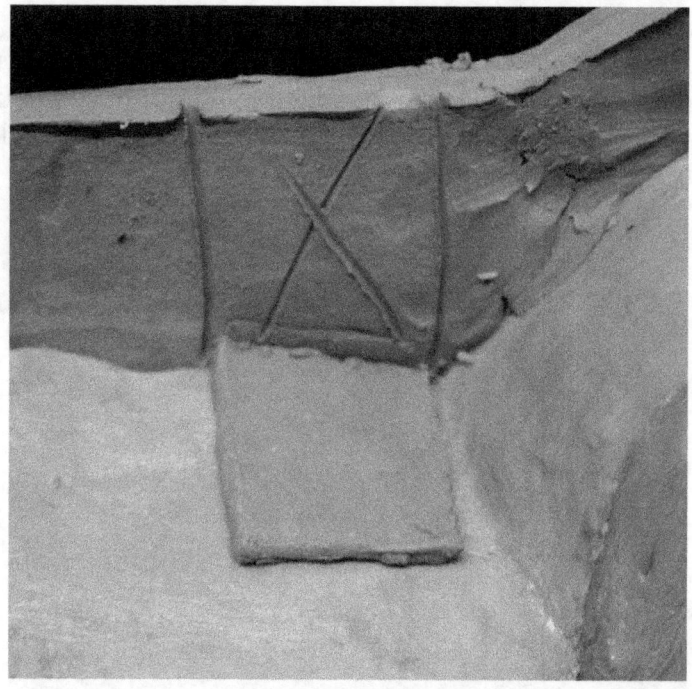

DIAGRAM 60

NOTE: Make sure the pry marks contact your clay wall. If they don't there will be a plaster barrier preventing you from putting your pry tools in and from doing their job.

Building the Second Half of the Mold

Here, we repeat all the same steps we went through making the first half. Once again, wear latex gloves and make sure you are wearing some sort of respirator as you build the four layers all over again.

Rather than rewriting those steps and adding unnecessary length to the book I am going to ask that you return to the following sections for instructions. Please repeat sections;

- Plaster Layer 1: The First Splash Coat
- Plaster Layer 2: The Second Splash Coat
- Plaster Layer 3: The Insurance Layer
- Plaster Layer 4: The Protective Layer

Once you have repeated those sections, applying the information to side two of the mold, you may advance to Step 5: Demolding.

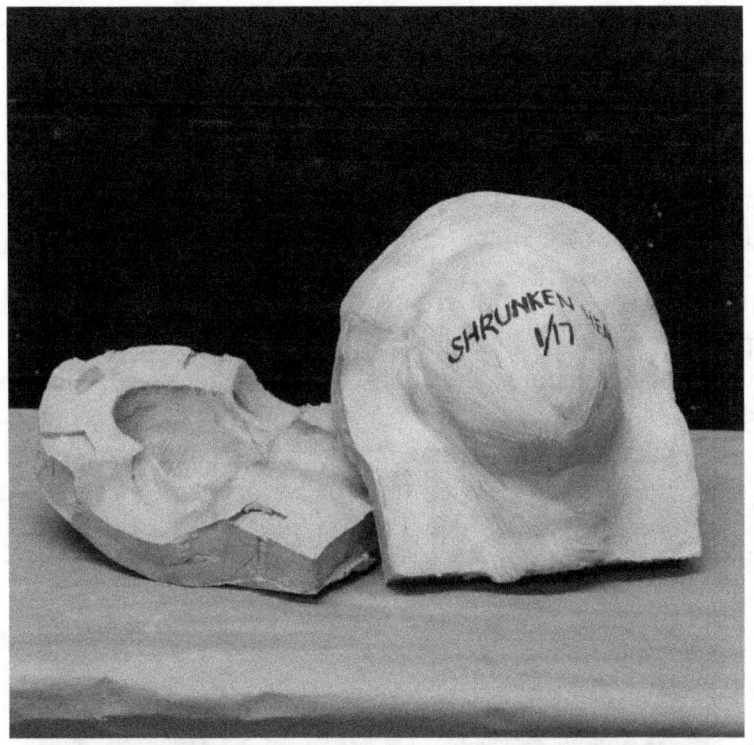

STEP 5: DEMOLDING

Demolding Materials

1. Water
2. Wooden mixing sticks (For removing clay)

Tools

1. Work gloves
2. Rasp (or file)
3. Chip brush
4. Small pry bar

5. Spray bottle

Set the mold upright on your work surface. Clear away all the extra materials such as 2X4s, scrap clay, sculpting tools, and other debris that might be hanging around. All you should have on hand is your mold and the materials listed above.

Remove the clay wall from the side of the mold. This will reveal the plaster caseline of the second half of the mold. Now, grab a rasp or file and clean up the edges of the plaster mold. This stuff gets sharp, so be careful and wear work gloves for protection. You just want to round off the corners so you don't get cut up. Use the chip brush to dust off the surface of the plaster mold after you are done filing down the edges. You don't want plaster bits getting into the mold as you pry it apart.

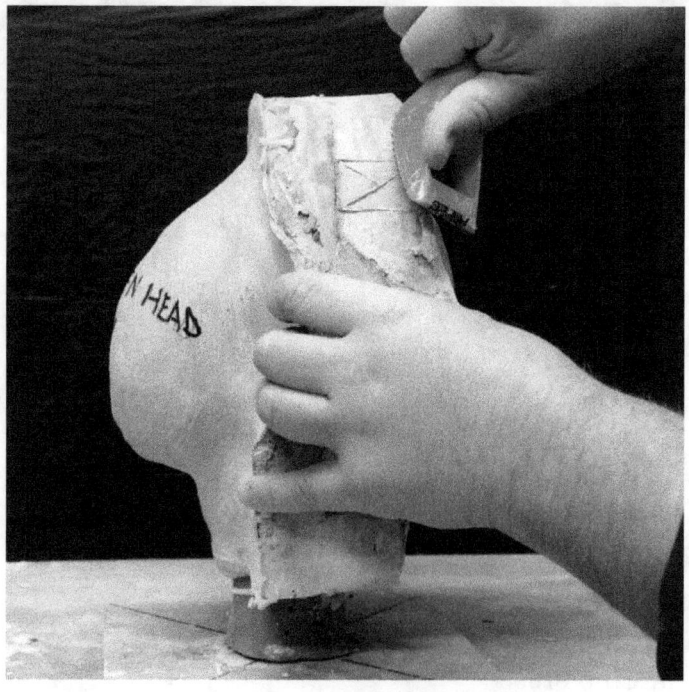

DIAGRAM 61

Do you recall those lines we scratched on the inside of the clay wall, above the pry marks? Locate those lines on the mold. They won't be indented now, they will look like mound lines on the plaster. Once you find them, insert your pry bar carefully yet forcibly into the clay pry marks, squishing out the clay as the pry bar sinks in.

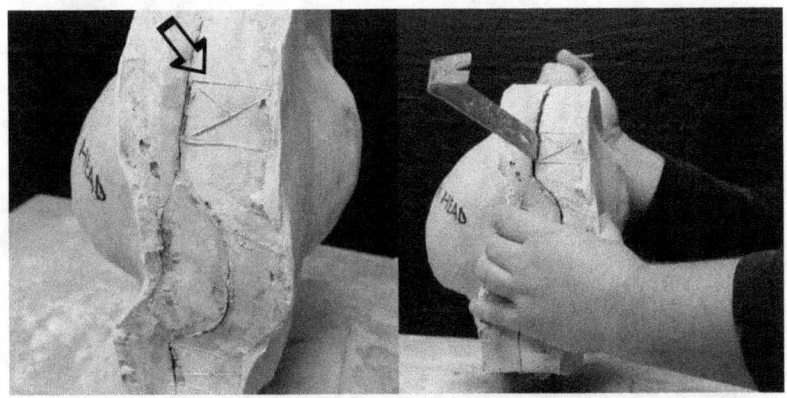

DIAGRAM 62

Remember when I said thin pry slots are good? The thin space forces the caseline open simply by inserting a pry bar. If you don't have pry bars you can use two large flathead screwdrivers, but be gentle so you don't crack the plaster.

Now gently pry the two mold halves apart, making sure you apply equal pressure to both sides of the mold so you preserve its integrity.

Pry bars are the preferred tool for this, because they are wider and spread out the force applied while prying against the plaster. A screwdriver has a smaller surface space, which focuses that force in a smaller area, increasing the odds that you will break your mold. I highly suggest you get some pry bars from Harbor Freight or a local dollar store.

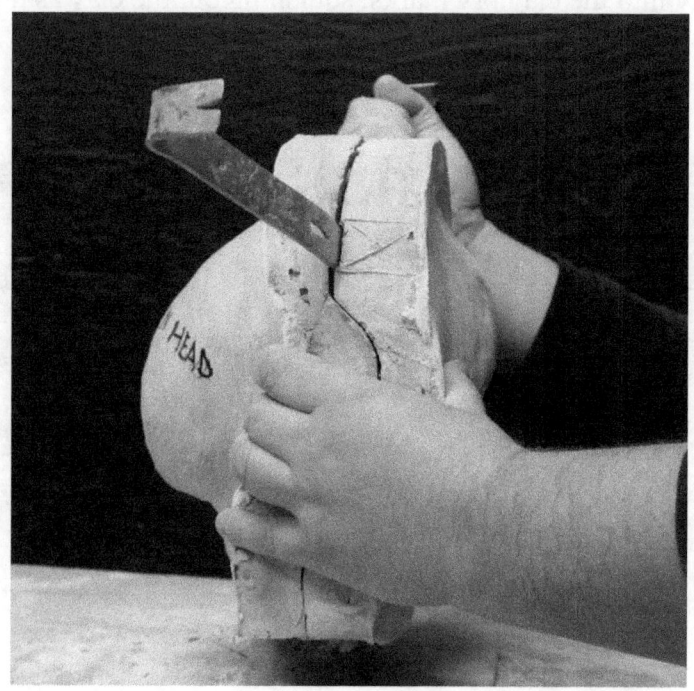

DIAGRAM 63

You will start to see the mold opening once you slide the pry bars in place. If you do, pat yourself on the back. If the mold is opening that is a really good thing.

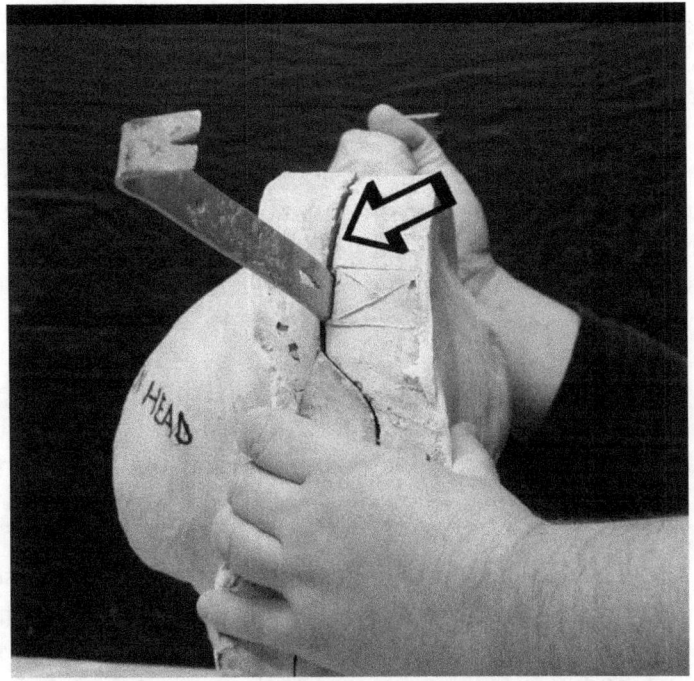

DIAGRAM 64

Work the bottom pry marks as well as the top ones. Make sure if you have a pry bar in the lower right pry mark you also have one in the lower left pry mark. Alternate between the bottom and top pries until you get the mold open enough to pull the mold apart by hand.

It's common for the back of the mold to come completely off the sculpture first. The front will sometimes be a pain to remove. You may need to use a wooden mixing stick to clear away some of the clay between the armature and the mold. It may take a while. What you have is vacuum pressure from the wet clay holding the two pieces together. It is pretty common. Don't rush.

Clear away some clay from the areas I suggested and from time to time try to dislodge the armature by pulling on it or the mold. You want to use some force, but not so much you could break the mold. In this case, the armature is expendable. It's really just a wooden dowel and some foil. Break it if you need to. Eventually they will come apart. In a pinch, you could use a little water pressure to erode the clay. I suggest nothing stronger than a garden hose…minus the spray nozzle. DON'T TAKE IT TO A CAR WASH!

> **FUN FACT:** I had a friend with this brilliant idea. Rather than do the work and clean out the mold by hand, he decided to take it to a car wash. We had been working on a film and we were already behind because the director changed the design of the creatures about two weeks before the day. In case you don't know, The Day, is the phrase we in the film community use to refer to the day of shooting. My buddy, a lazy and stupid-stupid-stupid man, headed to a local car wash. His plan was to brace the mold to keep it from moving while he used the high-pressure water to remove the clay. It worked like a charm. Or so he thought.
>
> The clay came flying out of the mold. He was ecstatic…until the water was turned off. Turns out the mold had an air bubble, or so we gathered. When the high-pressure water hit the mold, it punched through that thin plaster splash coat, exposing an air hole. It didn't stop there. The pressure must have forced the surrounding splash coat to peel away. More and more of the plaster was ripped out.
>
> When he shut the water off he started to see flecks of gray plaster bits all over the stall, like confetti at a parade. Upon inspection of the mold, he discovered

there was no detail left in it. The moron had ripped most of it out.

Had he cleaned the mold out properly we would have discovered the air pocket and fixed it. Hell, the plaster might have held and we might have gotten several casts before it even became a problem. Instead we got to redo the entire thing.

You might get away with it once, maybe twice. At some point, it's going to catch up with you and screw up a week's worth of work. The moral of the story is don't be a lazy idiot. Clean the mold out the right way.

Once the mold is apart and your armature is tucked out of the away, clean all the clay out of the mold—i.e., your sculpture. Use wooden tools to remove the clay instead of metal ones, because wooden tools are less likely to scratch the surface of your mold. You can use water to help break down the clay.

DON'T USE YOUR SCULPTING TOOLS FOR A CLEAN-OUT! The process will destroy your newly created wooden tools. Instead, use the wooden mixing sticks to remove the clay mess.

You can't save your sculpture without damaging the mold, so don't even try. But you can save a lot of the clay for reuse if you are careful. Once you have removed the clay, use a toothbrush or a chip brush and warm water to clean out any residue.

This cleanout will take a while, so be patient. If mold making is evil, then the cleanout is its baby brother. It sucks, but it's part of the gig.

Russ Adams

There might be a moment when you think you have it all cleaned out. I am betting you don't. If you think you do, walk away from the project for a day and let the plaster dry. Come back the next morning and spray some water into the mold surface. That darker stuff is clay. Get it out of there.

If everything looks good, pat yourself on the back. Well done! If not, start over again at Step 1 and consider this lost project a learning experience. You didn't fail if you learned something.

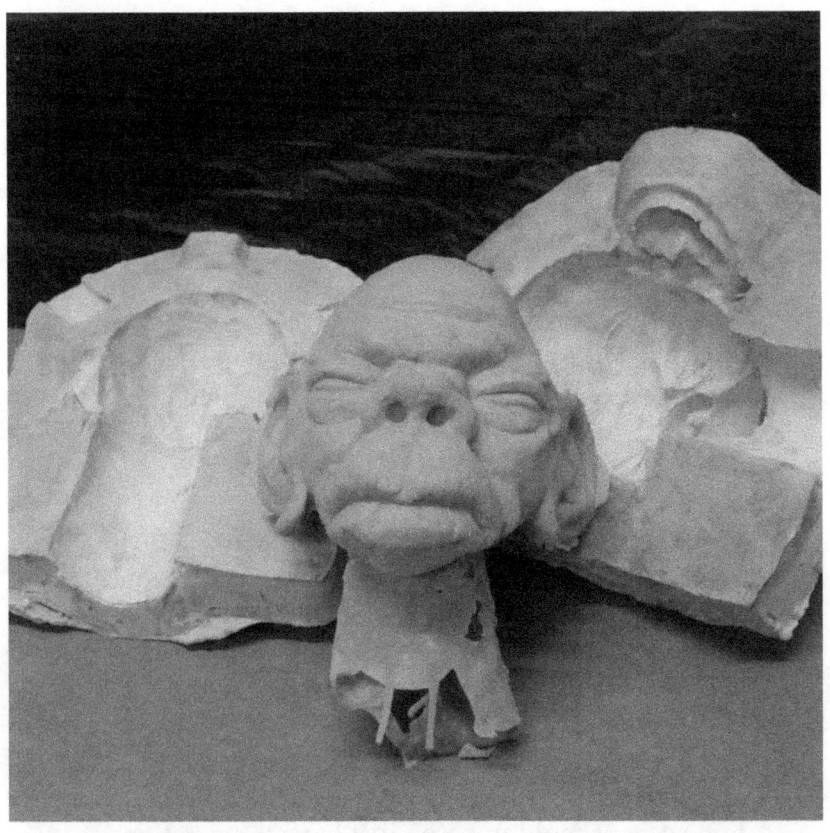

STEP 6: LATEX CASTING

Casting Materials

1. 1 gallon of Mask Latex
2. Mold straps (at least one)
3. Clear ammonia (optional)

Tools

1. Mold straps
2. Chip brush

3. Dremel tool
4. Clear ammonia (optional)

Let your mold halves dry for at least a week before trying to cast. The mold maybe cured, but it's not dry. The mold works by pulling the water out of the latex. If the mold isn't dry, then it can't pull any water out and you will be left with a horrible mess on your hands. (DON'T ATTEMPT TO SPEED THE MOLD-DRYING PROCESS BY BAKING OR HEATING THE MOLD. All you will do is crack or weaken it.)

> **FUN FACT:** We often use molds like these for foam latex makeup appliances, where you have to gently bake the foam latex in the mold. One day, after a long cool-down process—about 3 hours—I took a mold out of a 90-degree oven into a 75-degree work space. I got all of two feet away from the oven when I heard a gut-wrenching pop. That 15-degree difference in heat turned a week of work to trash within a tenth of a second. You don't need to heat your mold up. You just have to be patient!

When it's finally time to cast, put your mold halves together and secure them with mold straps. You can buy them for a few dollars at a ceramics supply store or a hobby store, and you might even find them on Amazon. They are a wise investment at three or four dollars.

I don't have a creative replacement for them. They are the best tool for the job. Don't try using rubber bands or cargo straps. The rubber bands stretch, and if your mold is big enough the weight of the latex can stretch them out enough to leak material everywhere. The latches on a cargo strap tends to put a focused strain on the mold and can crack it. Seriously, this is one of those tools you want to buy. Use the money you saved by not purchasing your tools.

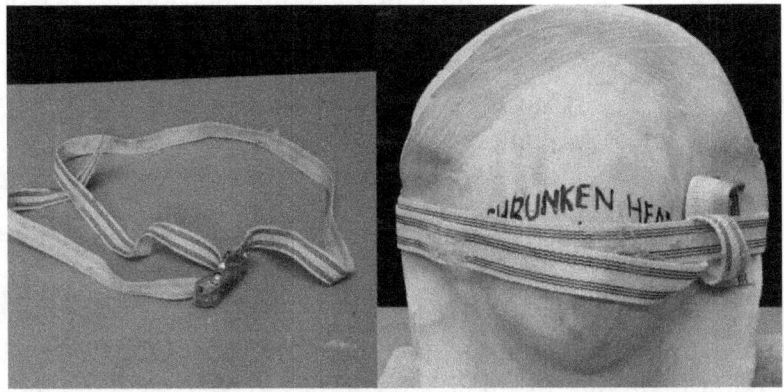

DIAGRAM 65

Once the mold is locked tightly together with the mold straps, set it on a work surface with the neck hole facing up. Slowly pour your latex into the neck of the mold, tapping the sides of the mold with the palm of your hand to disengage any air bubbles that form.

The latex should flow out a bit thicker than milk but not quite as thick as a milkshake. It certainly shouldn't plop out in globs. If it is too thick we can fix it. The PRO TIP below will explain.

> **PRO TIP:** When latex has been sitting for a few weeks, or even months, it will start to lose water and thicken up. This thicker latex is a pain to pour into a mold. It doesn't so much flow into the mold as it plops in. The thicker material also allows air bubbles to become trapped. They

can't escape through the thicker material and they tend to hang out in places that will ruin your day.

To revitalize your latex, add some clear ammonia to the mix. About a capful to a gallon at first. Mix the ammonia into the latex. If it thins the material out enough to get a more user friendly pour, then great. If not, add another capful. You don't want to overdo it, though.

I suggest getting the clear ammonia from the cleaning aisle at the dollar store. If might take you years to use it all, but it good to have nearby for latex work.

I usually pause when I have filled the mold about halfway. At this point I will turn the mold a few times to coat the entire inner surface of the mold with liquid latex. Then I continue filling the mold to the neck line.

Fill the mold completely. Give it about 15-20 minutes. You can even go to 45 mins, but that's a really thick shrunken head. Pour the remaining latex back into the pail. Place two pieces of wood under the mold with the neck hole facing down (see Diagram 66). Then go away and do something else while the latex solidifies and drains.

I let the mold drain for about twenty to thirty minutes, then close my bucket of latex and set the mold on the bench to dry overnight.

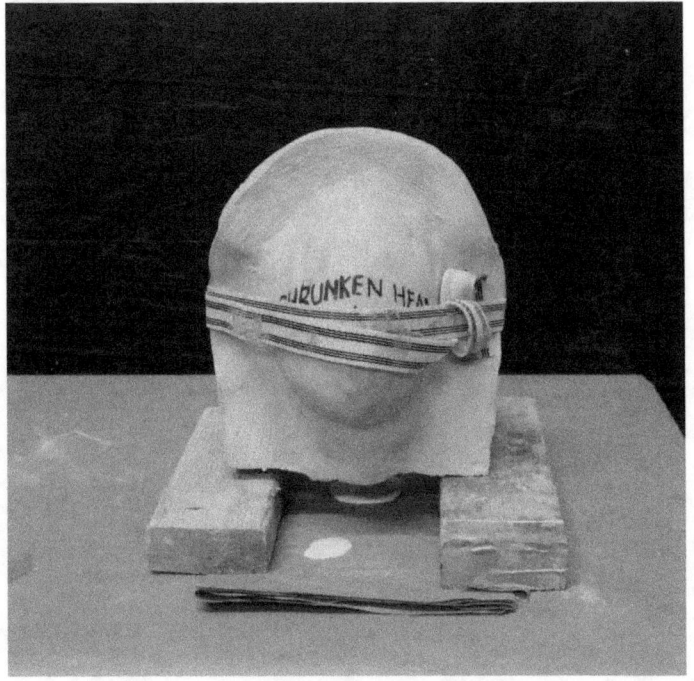

DIAGRAM 66

In the summer, you should be able to demold your cast the next morning. If it's spring or fall, you might have to wait another day. In the winter, you're more likely to wait two or three days. It depends on how long you let your mold dry and the temperature and humidity in the workspace.

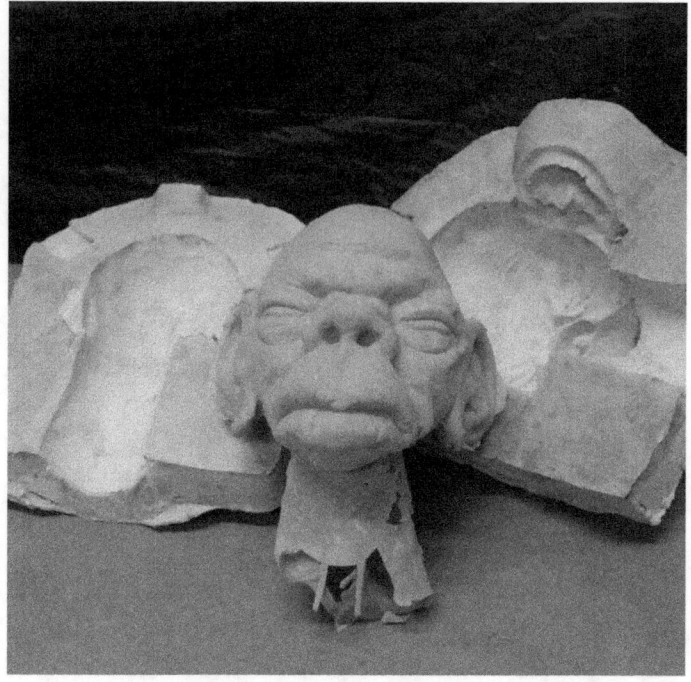

DIAGRAM 67

When the latex is dry, remove the mold straps, and use your pry bars to gently pry the mold open. Once again, remember to apply equal pressure on both sides of the mold. Once the mold halves are apart, you can peel out your latex cast and get it ready for cleaning and seam work. (Casts are also referred to as "pulls.")

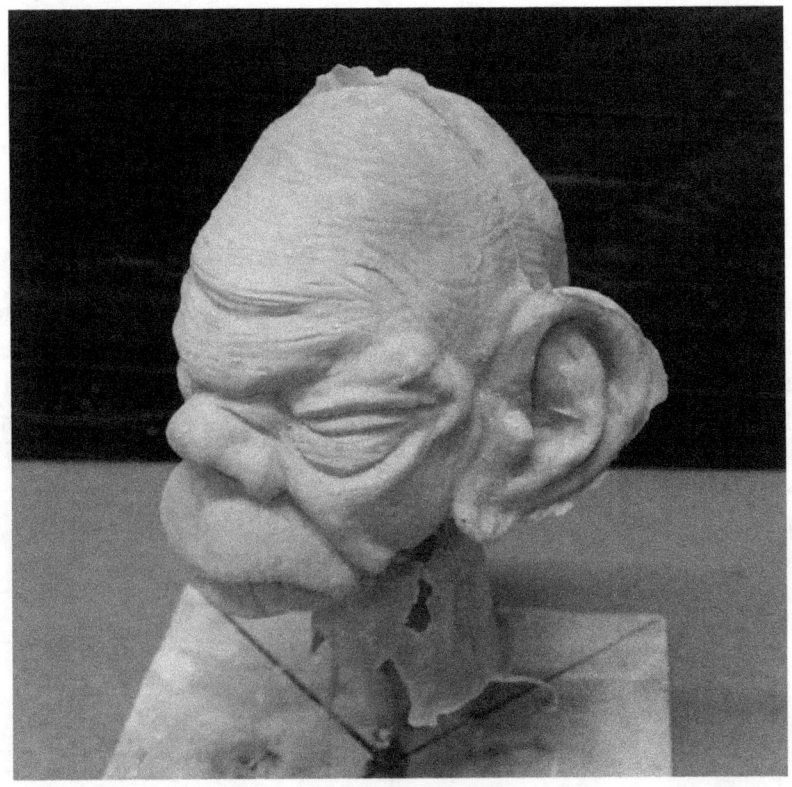

STEP 7: SEAMING & CLEANING

Seaming and Cleaning Materials

1. Latex and Cabosil Mixture (Cabopatch)
2. Mixing sticks
3. Mixing cup

Tools

1. Fingernail scissors
2. Dremel tool
3. Dremel stone or buffing bit
4. Chip brush

Completing your shrunken head involves seaming, cleaning, and various kinds of finishing. You might not think so, but these are very important steps. We will patch air bubble issues that might have occurred. We will clean up the seams that are caused by the caseline and remove the debris on the latex before we move onto the finishing work. Skip these steps and your work of art will suffer.

Seaming

Seaming is the art of removing any excess material left behind in the casting process, grinding down the evidence of that material, and filling in any holes or mishaps with raw latex and cabosil (also called cabopatch).

The first thing you may notice when you remove your cast from the opened mold is a thin line of extra material around the whole piece as seen in Diagram 68. This is called "flashing."

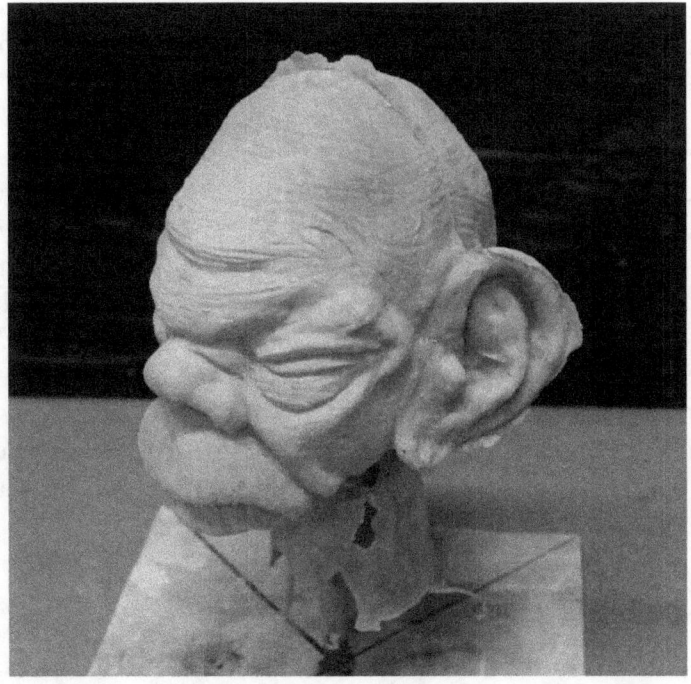

DIAGRAM 68

Basically, flashing is what happens when the straps don't hold the mold together tightly enough or there was debris on the caseline of the mold, which prevented it from closing completely. In more serious cases, the problem could be related to a poor mold construction. In all of these cases, the flashing is caused by a gap between the caselines that allowed liquid latex to leak between the two mold halves. It's a common thing to happen with a mold, especially a first mold.

On the plus side, if you have a latex pull that came out of your mold and didn't have a ton of latex leaking onto the floor, then you have a successful project. We just have to tune up your skills a bit, but that comes with practice.

Flashing can be removed with a pair of sharp scissors. I know I keep talking about making your tools not buying them, but this is where that money you saved can be well invested. I use Tweezerman Fingernail Scissors to remove the flashing. These are great scissors and I only use them on latex—nothing else. Tweezerman Scissors will set you back twenty-five to thirty-five dollars, but they do a great job and last a long time. I have had mine roughly four years or more. I bought my own after using them for the first time on the set of *Jim Henson's Creature Shop Challenge*. I was sold then and there. You can buy less expensive fingernail scissors to do the job, but in my experience, I was replacing them within a few weeks. In defense of the cheaper scissors, I do use them a lot, but the Tweezerman scissors have taken the same beating and stood the test of time.

And no, they aren't paying me a dime to say that.

The reason I use fingernail scissors is because of the curve. I use that curve to follow the contour of the mask's surface. You don't want to get too close to the mask when you are removing the flashing. Too close and you could cut deep enough to create a hole in the mask. So, leave about 1/16 of an inch behind and we will grind off the rest.

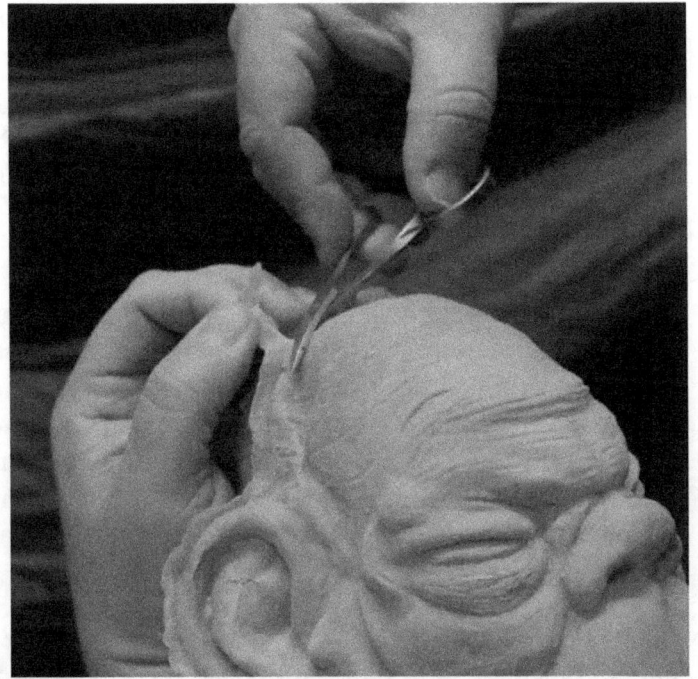

DIAGRAM 69

Seaming tutorial: www.youtube.com/watch?v=0w4_lEi4xGU

Once you remove the flashing, the seam can be ground away using a Dremel tool and either a stone bit or a buffing bit. If I use a stone bit, I use a round stone bit. I mostly use a buffing bit for this, but it's a personal preference, not quality related.

I set the Dremel on a medium speed and gently grind away the seam using a small circular pattern. It's important to take your time and be vigilant. There are two major problems that could occur when you are grinding off the seam.

141

1. You could grind the seam down too far with your Dremel. This might wear a hole in the surface of the shrunken head. This might even occur because you hit an unforeseen air bubble trapped in the latex. If this does happen don't panic. You can fill the hole with Cabopatch. Let the patch dry and use the Dremel to smooth the surface. Always let the Cabopatch dry completely before grinding off the rough area.

2. This is perhaps the most damaging issue to deal with when using a Dremel to remove seams from a shrunken head. Sometime your project can get wrapped around the Dremel. It happens when you set the Dremel speed too high and the latex catches the bit, and before you can react the latex is coiled around the Dremel bit. If this happens it can, and often does cause irreparable damage to the project. When the latex wraps up like this it stretches and twists the latex so badly that the latex often times won't rebound. So, to decrease the chances of having this happen to you, set the Dremel to a medium speed. Yes, it takes longer to finish the seaming, but at least you aren't sacrificing the shrunken head to the rotary-tool gods.

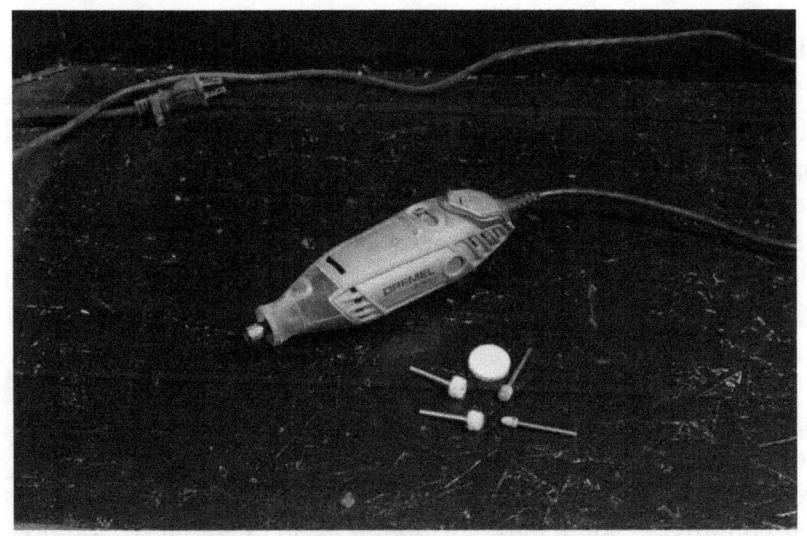

DIAGRAM 70

Cleaning

Cleaning is next. When you remove a pull (or cast) from a mold, especially a plaster mold, the cast often has plaster dust on the latex. It's actually part of your mold that has been pulled away by the latex. This is common and the reason why plaster molds have a limit to the number of pulls they can produce. With each pull, the mold loses a little more detail and material. So just be prepared.

This plaster debris needs to be scrubbed off the cast so you can paint the project. The other material that might very well be present is clay. It might be as simple as clay dust or it might be that you missed some clay during the mold cleanout. If you do have a chunk of clay in your shrunken head, go ahead and remove it. It may have left a hole or cavity in your project. Go ahead and use the Cabopatch to fix it. You will have to wait for the Cabopatch to dry completely before you clean the shrunken head, but that's part of the charm of these heads.

I use dish soap and a chip brush to clean the surface of a project. I cut down the bristles of the chip brush by about half. This makes the brush stiffer and helps to get the surface good and clean. I scrub the cast thoroughly, then put it on a hook to dry.

> **NOTE:** You don't need to soak the shrunken head. You only want to dampen the surface. If you get it too wet, it will make drying it difficult. It will still dry out, but it might warp the shape or take days.

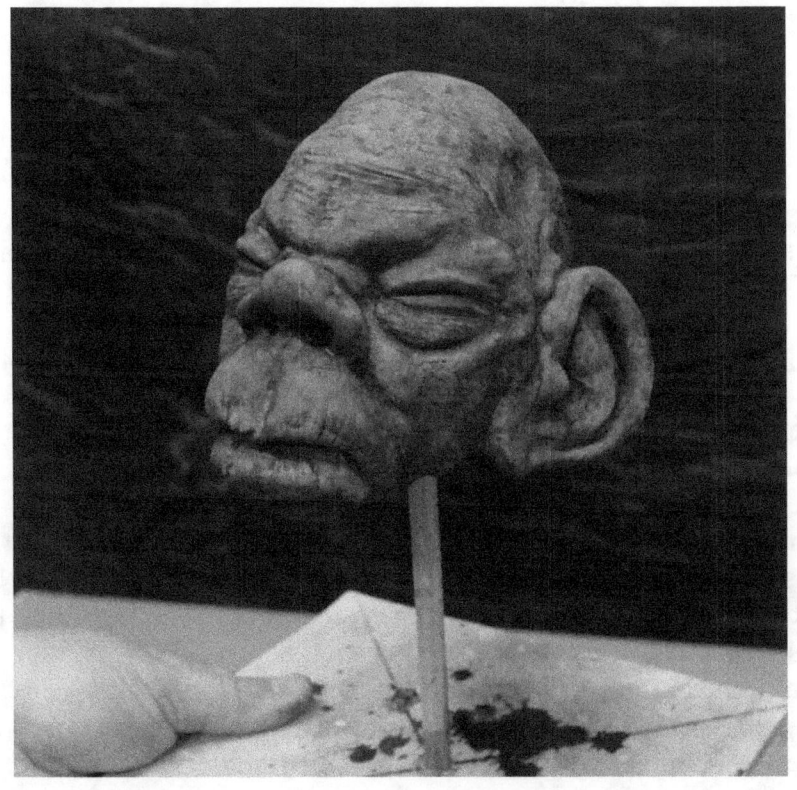

STEP 8: PAINTING

Painting Materials

1. Assorted paint (black, raw umber, tans, brown)
2. Water
3. Cabosil

Tools

1. Paint brushes
2. Sponges

3. Rinsing cup
4. Reference photos

When making a shrunken head, there are two fun stages and one pain in the butt. Sculpting is a blast—it's a process you can get lost in and really enjoy. Molding is the pain. You have to do it. It's a necessary evil. Finishing, on the other hand is the most fun of all. It's the whole process of painting, furring, and adorning your creation, or transforming it from a raw latex pull into a finished thing of beauty. Well, beautiful creepiness.

Before you start painting your shrunken head, seriously study your photo references and think about how real shrunken heads were made by those Amazonian tribes in Peru and Ecuador. Think about raw skin drying in smoke. It's going to collect soot. It's going to caramelize like a pig roasting on a spit. There will be more black and dark brown patches on the skin. And it's going to lose colors that a living human face would have. The reds, the pinks, the purples—those will be gone. The blood that makes living tissue blush will have boiled away and then roasted out of the skin. No more ruddy-colored lips or rosy cheeks.

With that lovely thought in mind, start your painting with a base color wash. The natural color of the latex works in your favor because it looks a bit like rawhide. What's human skin but our very own all-natural untanned leather.

We are going to use a few washes to stain the latex. Make sure your latex gloves are handy, because this is going to be messy.

I use one of two colors for a wash that will stain the latex. If I want a more burnt look, I use black. If I want a more roasted look, I use dark browns, like a raw umber. Browns and blacks are your best bet. Again, avoid reds. That means no red-browns either. Burnt umber and the like have enough red in them to make your gaff look like a gaff.

Washes

I will often do a two-parts water to one-part acrylic paint to create my washes. I use a chip brush to apply the wash, ensuring the entire pull is covered. Then I use a damp sponge, or cloth to dab off the paint.

I take great care to dab—never wipe. Wiping always removes too much and disturbs any natural look the washes create. I will hang the head on a hook to dry. Once it dries, I add another wash, and repeat.

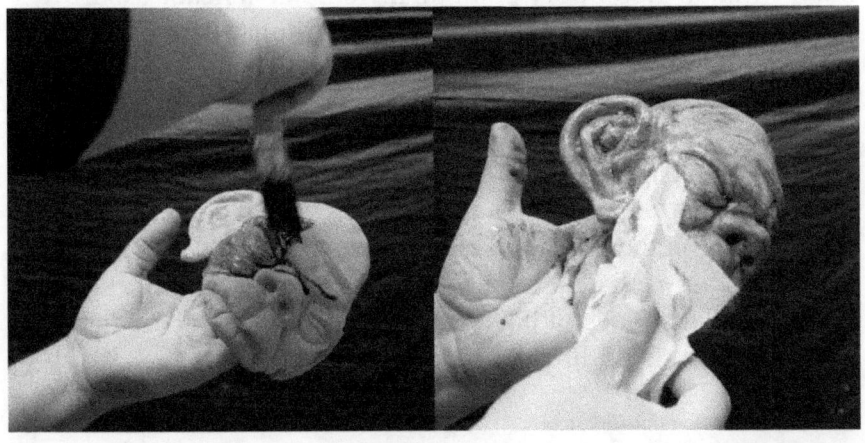

DIAGRAM 71

Highlights & Shadows

I want to hit the highlights and the shadows next. Let's start with the highlights. This might sound silly to some, but there may be some people who don't know where to put the highlights. Here is a simple test to show you where to highlight your creature. Set the shrunken head on your workbench. Look straight down at it. You see the tips of the ears, crown of the head, brows, tip of the nose, tops of the cheeks, upper lip, etc.

I want my highlights to look natural, so I am going to stagger them. I mix up a color that is a couple shades brighter than what is already there. This isn't a wash, but will be a bit watered down. I don't want a glob of dry paint on my shrunken head. Using a torn piece of a sponge (material left over from a foam fabrication project) as a paint brush of sorts, I will apply this slightly lighter color. I will start with the brow. I always do…not sure why.

I will dab the paint on the area of the brow, one eyebrow at a time. I say that because the paint tends to dry on one side while I am working on the other side. Once the paint is dabbed on the brow I will immediately knock it back with another piece of sponge, one that doesn't have paint on it. I will then beat the paint down further with a chip brush.

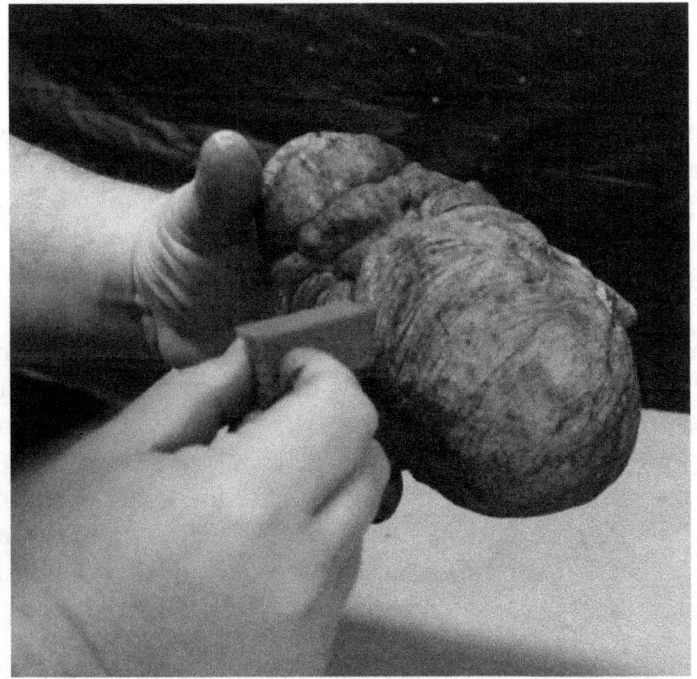

DIAGRAM 72

Why a sponge with a rough edge? The rough edge is imperfect. I don't want there to be a solid area of paint. I want it to mottle. The subtle and rough torn edge adds an uneven and chaotic distribution of paint to the area of focus. I like that it does this because uniformity, in the case of my character, is not ideal.

I will repeat this process in all the areas I mentioned, then move to a slightly brighter version of the same colors. Two colors, each a couple shades brighter than the last, should do the trick. But you should do more or less depending on what you want from your creature.

For the second highlight color, I will reduce the area where I add paint, perhaps fifty percent less space than I covered on the first highlight color. I will use the same process as before to apply and knock down the tones.

Now the darker areas, the shadows. If you aren't sure where these areas are, simply turn the project upside down and look straight down on it. The areas under the chin, jawline, backs of the ear-lobes, under the nose, under the brow, recesses of the eyes, etc. are the shadows.

The shadows are really a repeat of the highlights only with a darker paint. My plan is to employ the same process using the sponges. Don't go crazy with this either. I am only going to use two colors and blend it out. For instance, I will start with the area below the chin. The plan is to add paint to the wider portion of the chin toward the jawline, then knock it back with the sponge. When I come back to this area with the second color, I will focus more in the center of the chin, and not in those border areas.

Speckling

I am a huge fan of speckling. After each color is applied, I use an old toothbrush or a modified chip brush with the bristles cut off at the halfway point to speckle my shrunken head. I dip the brush I am using into the wash or a washed-out version of each color I use to paint the shrunken head. I knock off a bit of the excess paint, point the brush at the head, and gently flick a spray of droplets at the surface of the head. I will do this all the way around the project.

On occasion, there will be a large spot on the surface that doesn't look right. While it's still wet, I will knock it down with my fingertip. Just tap it down. The color will remain but will be more diffused.

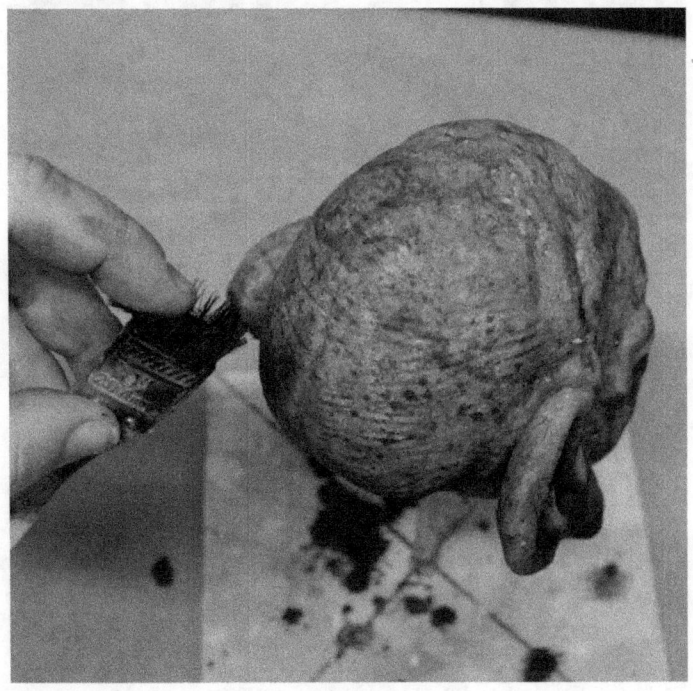

DIAGRAM 73

This flicking of colors adds a blotchy look, and simulates those tiny spots, moles, and freckles humans have on our skin. You can add colors to the mix. You aren't restricted to the colors you have used for the base paint. This is where you might get away with a hit of red-browns, and even blues.

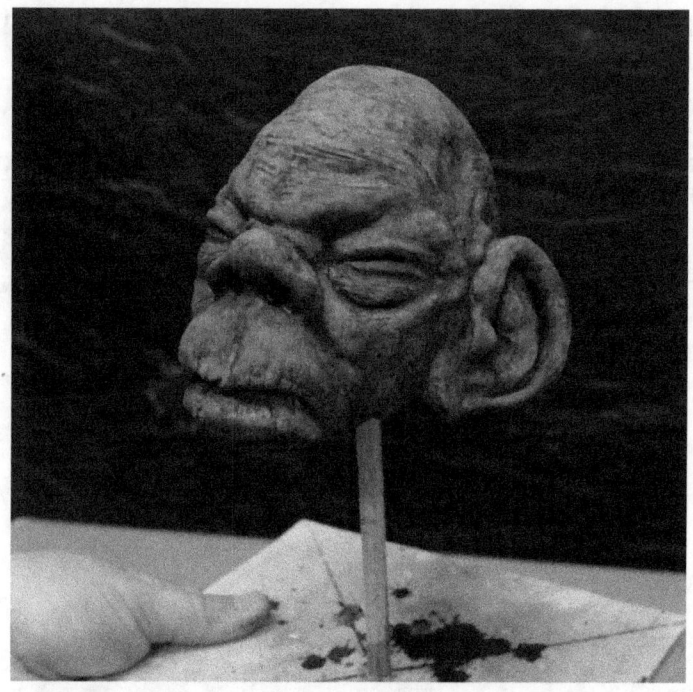

DIAGRAM 74

 I will also shade the deeper pockets of the face, eye orbits, inner ear, nose, and mouth with a darker grey. I might even chase it with some blue/black.

Each color I add will be followed by a flicking of that same color on the mask in the same way described earlier. There may be more of one color and less of another, but the process will continue until I am done painting.

Russ Adams

Fluid Stains

It's a gross concept, these fluid stains, but they are a realistic add. Think about what we talked about during the section called A Short History of Shrunken Heads. The practitioners boiled the face sack, then dried it over smoke and hot coals. We talked about the eruption from fluid escaping the skin and how it must have run down the face, boiling on the surface of the skin. The fluid trails would have stained streaks onto several areas of the victim's face. Having them on our shrunken head adds a gory and realistic detail.

I have always found that the best way to mimic a fluid stain is to use thin paint, like our washes. I just let an excess build up until the paint runs. I will let this roll down the face and I won't defuse it. It will dry as is.

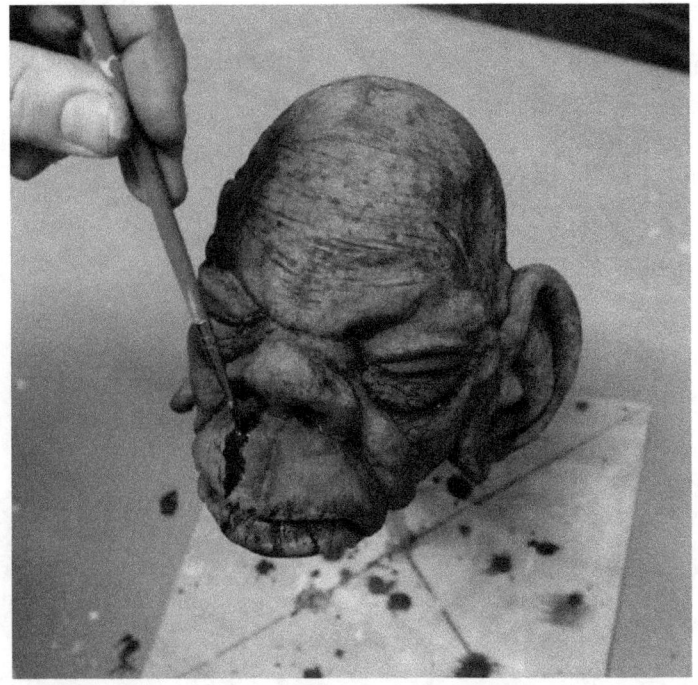

DIAGRAM 75

I will deliberately put too much paint in the ear canals and then coax it to run out, after which gravity deserves all the credit. You don't want the runoff to look perfect. Water is somewhat unpredictable as it scurries down a surface. Don't believe me, watch the water run down your skin the next time you get into the shower. It often changes direction, and in some very odd paths.

If the runoff is too dark or thick I will intervene. When this happens, I give the paint a second or two to stain the surface, and then chase it with a sponge…again, dabbing at it rather than wiping.

I use the same method with respect to eye sockets, mouth, and nostrils. These areas are likely spots for the moisture to have evacuated and stained the skin before it ran off the face like river tributaries.

The fact that I think about these things must say a great deal about me in real life.

War Paint

War paint, or tribal adornments, is one of my favorite steps of the process. I get to search the internet for all the different variations of tribal face painting. Most of them are breathtaking. And the colors are dazzling—reds, yellows, blues, whites, blacks, and blended combinations of all. They are a blast to look at, and to replicate.

I like to go truly rustic with my war paints. When I find a paint scheme I am fixated on, I like imagine how that pigment was devised. Chalky pastes come to mind. So, when I mix my paint I add material to it, such as Cabosil. Cabosil is a thickening agent. We used it to thicken up raw liquid latex to patch holes in the shrunken head in the Seaming and Cleaning section of this workshop. I am going to use it now to make my acrylic paint look more like a raw chalky pigment.

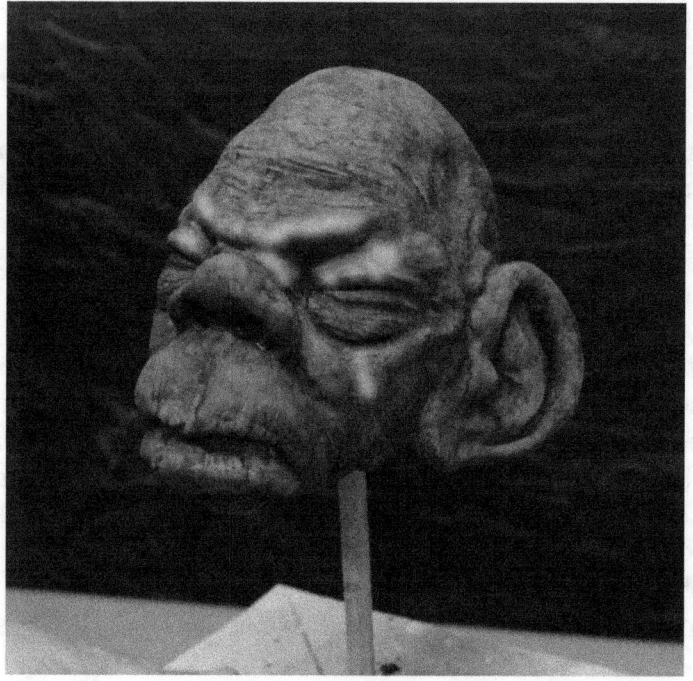

DIAGRAM 76

I also like to apply it rather roughly. I don't think for a second that these tribal artists are anything less than perfectionists. I am certain they take great pride in their work. Perfection doesn't fit into the esthetic of my design, though. While I don't want to offend them, I do have an agenda of my own. So, I will apply this haphazardly. I want it to look like this fella has been wearing the paint for a while. I want it haggard and running. I think it fits the vision I have for my shrunken head. You should do what fits into your design.

Once the paint dries we can move on to the next step. But you can see how one step truly builds upon the success of the last. From the initial washes to the war paint, all of these methods add a layer of detail to the painted portion of the shrunken head. If we were to leave the piece as is, it would look great. I don't want great. I want fan-freakin-tastic, so we still have some tricks to add to this sucker.

Russ Adams

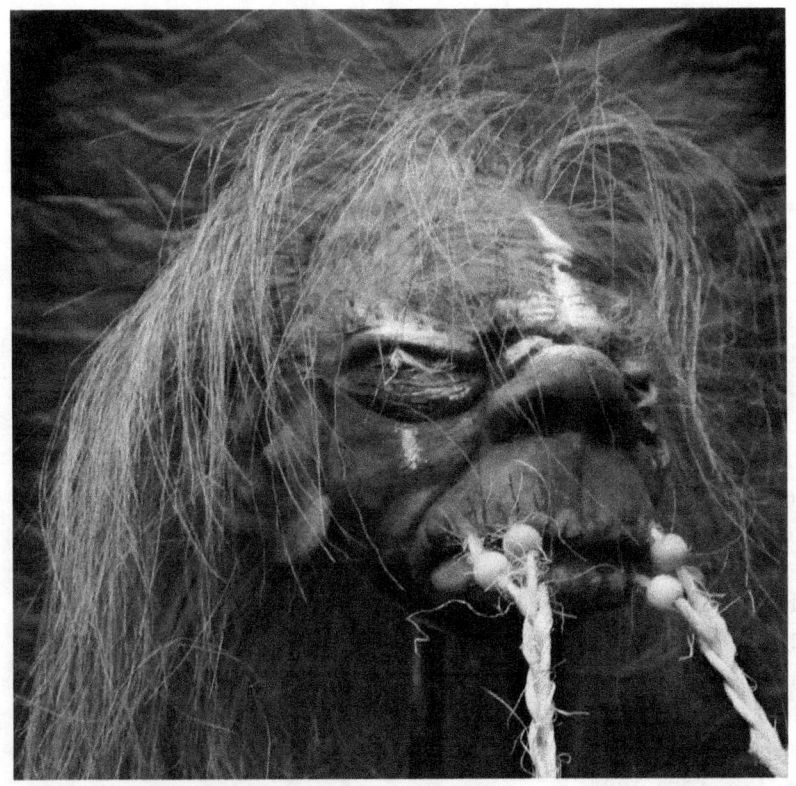

STEP 9: HAIR PUNCHING

Hair Punching Materials

1. Hair shanks
2. Superglue
3. A sewing machine needle
4. 3/8 wood dowel

Tool

1. A Dremel tool with a stone attachment
2. Eye protection
3. Drill and drill bit

4. A vise of some sort

The Basics

Hair punching is a process which uses a special needle to drive hairs into the surface of a finished piece. We essentially use a modified sewing machine needle to accomplish this. Some people use a felting needle, but those needles are really only effective with very soft materials like silicone. The majority of the hair punching I do is on latex skins and upholstery foam. It's much harder and will destroy the felting needles in the first few punches. In my opinion, using the modified sewing machine needle is the best option. It's strong enough to punch hair into latex and does a great job on silicone too.

The needle is designed to catch a hair or two in a fork that we create. The needle is then driven into the surface of a nearly finished piece of work. The most common materials we special-effects artists punch hair into are latex, silicone, and foam. The friction of the fake skin typically holds the hair in place as the needle is removed.

So, that's it in a nutshell.

Problems with Hair Punching

There are number of other methods you can use to put hair on a project, but this one gives the best results in my opinion. If you tried to glue the hair in or on your project, it could easily end up looking like one of those cheap dolls sold at the local dollar store although it can look good, if done well. But this is an art unto itself. Hair punching is much better, but also slower, because it is always done one or two strands at a time. It's mind numbing, but speed comes with practice and focus.

The other problem that slows thing down and adds some stress is when a tool breaks. Hair punch needles break—especially when punching into latex. To combat this, I always make a dozen needles and have them ready. Having extra needle on hand if I break one is good practice. This allows me to press on with the project without having to stop and make another needle. Few things are worse than derailing a hair punching rhythm simply to stop and make a new needle. So just make more than you think you will need and be prepared.

Hair Direction

The trick to hair punching is to start from the bottom and work your way up, always taking note of the hair direction. If you drive the hair in at the wrong angle, then the hair will stick straight out or look unnatural. The bedhead look is not desirable for most projects.

Drive the hair in at an upward angle to get a more natural look. The best place to get information on hair growth is from references.

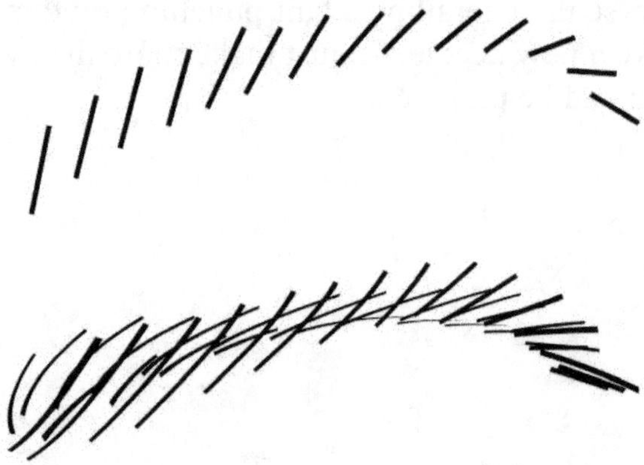

DIAGRAM 77

Reference Materials

You might recall that I discussed the importance of reference materials in the Sculpting section of this book. Reference photos are the key to a successful project. We tend to think a thing looks one way, but it is typically another. To stay focused on how something really looks, we use reference photos.

I will use a human eyebrow as an example. Most think of an eyebrow as a neat line of hair moving in one direction, usually horizontally over the brow, but it's not actually like that at all. The human eyebrow grows in many different directions and horizontal is but one minor route. Having a good clear extreme close-up of an eyebrow to refer back to as you work will allow you to create a more realistic eyebrow for your project.

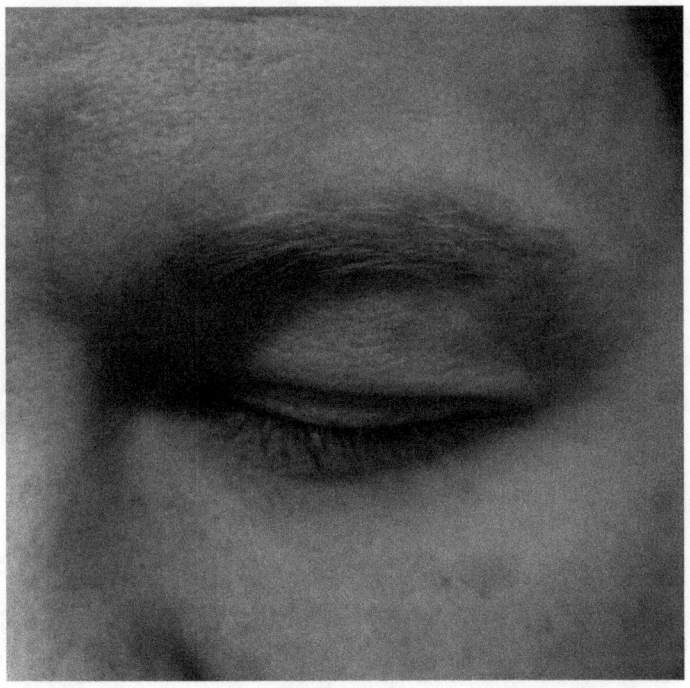

DIAGRAM 78

You may choose not to put eyebrows on your shrunken head. That in itself adds to your fella's backstory. No matter what you are doing, find a set of reference photos to help guide you and keep you rooted in the project. Rooted! I crack myself up.

Finding Hair

There are a lot of options for hair. You can buy shanks of crepe hair in various colors, or even reuse old wigs from Halloween. If I had to choose, I would go with crepe hair, but wigs are more readily available and you can often get them cheap if you don't already have one lying around.

Crepe is expensive, and it takes forever to straighten it. Crepe hair usually comes braided in a little package. It keeps the fine hairs from tangling and knotting up. This is one of those times where the cure is worse than the disease. You need a hackle or comb to work out the kinks and this could take an hour or better. Crepe hair is the best option of the two choices, in my opinion. I prefer to use high grade acrylic hair, yak, and/or mohair. But you could always gross someone out by using *real* human hair, too.

Here are a couple of places you can find your hair:

Crepe Hair: This can be purchased at www.fxsupply.com in a variety of colors.

Yak, Mohair, and High-Grade Acrylic Hair: These items can be purchased by the pound at www.nftech.com. You will pay a hefty sum, but it goes a long, long way and looks amazing.

Wigs: you can find wigs anywhere from www.amazon.com to a yard sale or one of those cheap big box stores.

Russ Adams

The Secret to Hair Punching

There are only a few tricks to hair punching—surface, process, stamina, and a sharp needle.

Surface

If your project is hollow, like our shrunken heads, I suggest you visit your local hobby/craft store to pick up a Styrofoam ball or scavenge some upholstery foam before you start hair punching your project. It should be large enough to fit tightly inside the project or at least big enough to create some surface tension when it's packed inside the shrunken head. Don't worry if the foam ball distorts the shape of the latex. You will be removing it as soon as the hair punching is complete. The latex will return to his original shape.

Surface tension is key when hair punching, especial with latex. When you are hair punching, you never want much flex in the surface. Flex equals a broken hair punch needle, which means time constructing new ones. Flex in the latex translates to a bend in the hair punching needle. Since these needles are very brittle they snap. Worse yet, you might end up injuring yourself. So, remember surface tension.

Process

Before you begin hair punching, you should have a plan for the hair pattern. Regardless of the pattern, you want to start at the lowest possible point, and work your way up. For example, if you are hair punching a beard, start at the neck, and work out and up. If it's a Mohawk, work from the bottom back of the hair line, and upward toward the forehead.

This is the most logical place to start. If you start at the top of the head and work backward you are going to be fighting to keep the hair you just punched out of your way. With every line of hair you punch in, there will be more and more hair to work against. So just start low and work upward.

If you look at Diagram 79 you can see that I am hair punching a Bigfoot Torso Mask ™. You can see how I not only start low and work my way up, but I also create imperfect lines. I will work from right to left on a particular section and then step up a sixteenth of an inch or so to the next line, and start working that area.

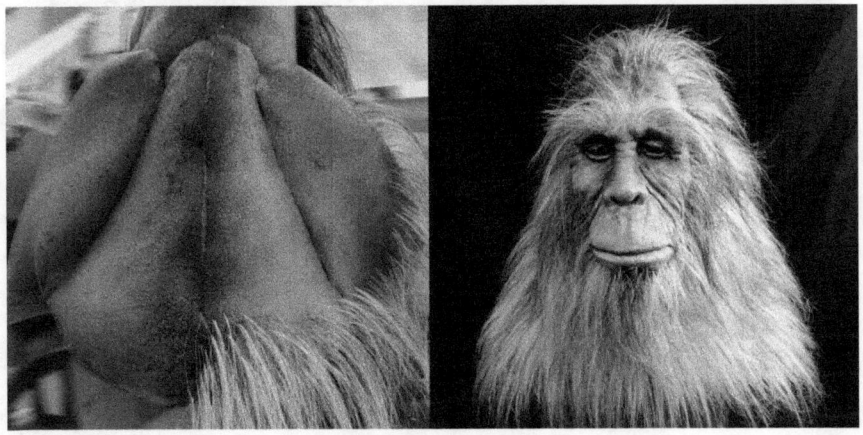

DIAGRAM 79

A word of advice…starting is the worst part of the process. I call
it Beginner's Hesitation. When I say "beginner" I mean
"beginning," not necessarily a novice. Beginner's hesitation
refers to those first few strands of hair we punch into a surface. It
can also apply to the first fine details we add to a sculpture, the
first spots we add to a paint job. It often looks stupid and causes
people to think they are doing it wrong. Those first few lines of
hair are going to look horrible because they are the first few lines.
Look at Diagram 80. Do you see how the hair changes as you go?
It eventually begins to look like you want. You must stay the
course. So, don't get sidetracked by Beginner's Hesitation.

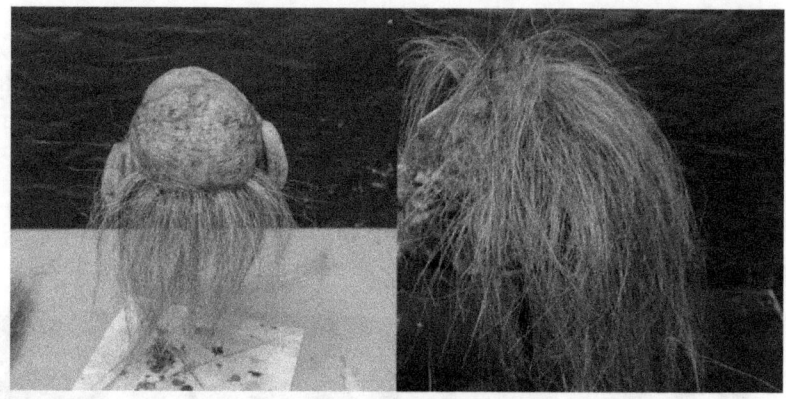

DIAGRAM 80

Stamina

Hair punching is exhausting and boring. If you feel yourself getting bored or rushing to finish, just step away for a short time. While you are away from your project, think of the artists here at Escape Design FX. We typically punch entire bodies and have a very short time to do it. Our Bigfoot suit took about a week of solid hair punching from the feet all the way up to the top of the head.

> **FUN FACT:** The Bigfoot suit was a solo build. It was all me. It took me an entire day to hair punch one of the Bigfoot creature boots at a marathon pace. I literally spent less time hair punching the Torso Mask ™. After I finished that first boot, I considered returning the clients' money before starting the next one. Hang in there. The end result is well worth the back pain, crossed eyes, and tears.

Seriously though, breaks are important. We tend to be less detail-oriented when we are fatigued. We rush through just to see it done and out of our sight. It's a common feeling, even among the professionals. Just step back. Get a cup of coffee. Go for a walk. If you can, maybe even come back to it the following morning. But whatever you do, don't sacrifice quality.

Sharp Needles

Sharp needles win the race. It's important to keep your needle sharp. Often, we punch foam suits while they are on the mannequin. We often hit the mannequin with the needle, dulling the point or bending the delicate fork with every impact. You can sharpen your needle with a Dremel or even sandpaper. My favorite tool to clean and sharpen needles is a sanding sponge. I whip the needle across it to sharpen the point, and repeatedly stab the sponge with the needle to clean it when adhesive builds up on the surface.

The most important thing is safety. Please be careful when you are hair punching. You can easily break a needle, or stick yourself with the tool. Everyone does at some point. Just be cautious and take your time.

Making a Hair Punch Needle

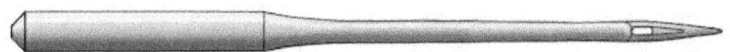

There is nothing special about this needle. All you need a common sewing machine needle like this one.

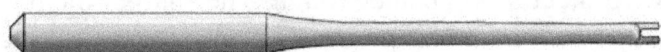

You will need to remove the point just above the "eye" of the needle using a sander or with a rotary tool like a Dremel. Use a stone attachment and grin the material away. Don't try to cut this with pliers or scissors. Take it slow.

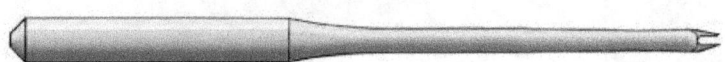

Using the Dremel and the stone attachment taper the ends of the needle's "eye." Again, go slowly. You can easily burn through the metal of the needle, ruining it completely. This "U" shaped fork is where we catch the strands of hair when we are hair punching.

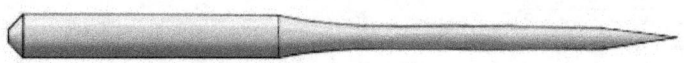

Turn the needle, and taper the front and back side of the needle's "eye." The reason we sharpen the sides and the front and back of the needle is so we get the best possible point. Piercing the surface of any project's skin can be rough. The sharper the point on the needle the better the hair punch. This also means having fewer broken needles.

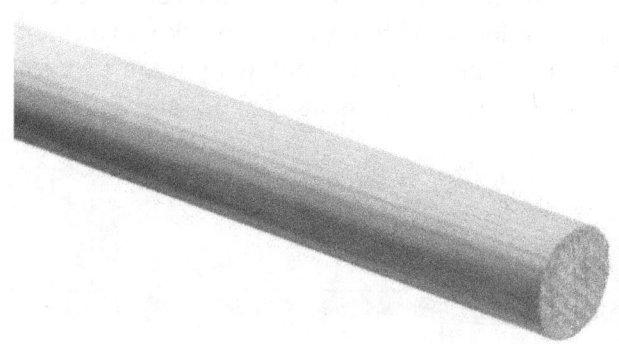

Next, cut a 3/8-inch diameter wooden dowel to about 3-4 inches in length. You may want to modify the length of the dowel in the future to accommodate your personal comfort.

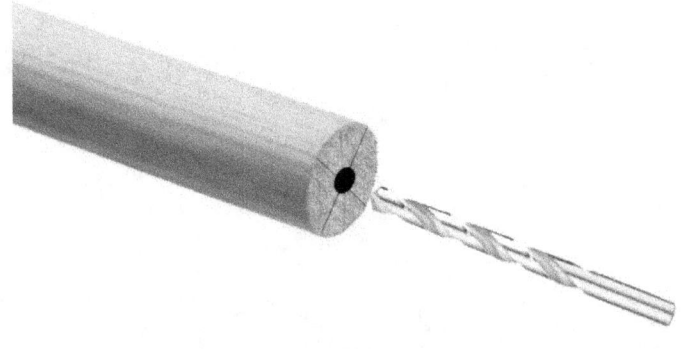

Find a drill bit that matches the diameter of your modified sewing machine needle. Mark the center of the dowel and drill a hole about a half-inch deep. I highly suggest you place the dowel into a clamp or vise before you drill into it. It may sound like a no-brainer but I have actually seen people attempt to drill this hole holding the dowel in their hand. A couple times people succeeded in drilling into their digits as well as the dowel. Please put the dowel into a vise.

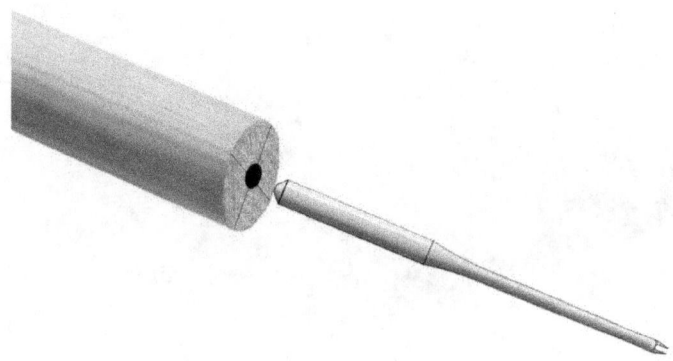

Place a drop of superglue in the dowel hole, then insert the modified sewing machine needle into the dowel. I use a pair of needle-nose pliers to force the end of the needle into the dowel. It makes the process so much easier.

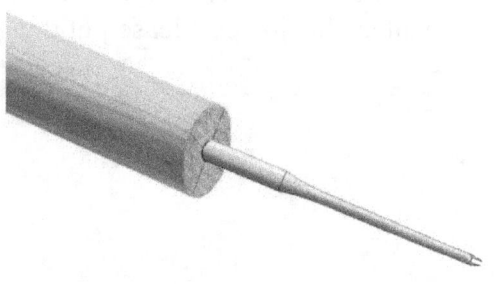

Congratulations! You've made a hair punch needle. Now make a few more and you can get started punching hair.

NOTE: Please take all safety precautions when making this tool. Wear eye protection. If you are under 18, make sure to have adult supervision.

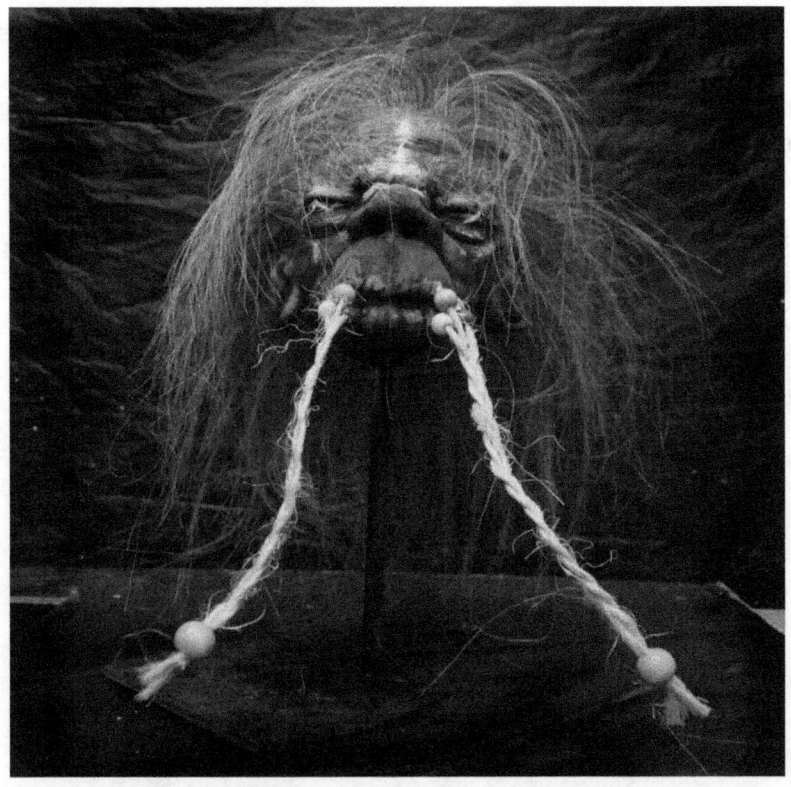

STEP 10: ADORNMENTS

Let talk about adornments for a second. This is just another layer of detail that transforms your creation from cool to mind-blowing. So, we want to take advantage of all this brings to our piece. What do you want to add to your shrunken head to make it pop?

We have talked about some of the things that happen to a shrunken head during the process. In one of those incredibly freakish developments, the practitioner sews the eyes and the mouth shut. Remember, you cannot find what you can't see. If you can't speak, you can't curse the practitioner for what he has done. Right now, you are the practitioner. You created this shrunken head and now you have to protect yourself from being cursed. So, what steps will you take?

I found some crazy uses of twine on shrunken heads while doing a little online recon. I found a couple in particular that I am going to implement on my victim's head. While I can't show you my references, I can show you my progress—for instance, I replicated these twine adornments by braiding the twine and adding some wooden beads.

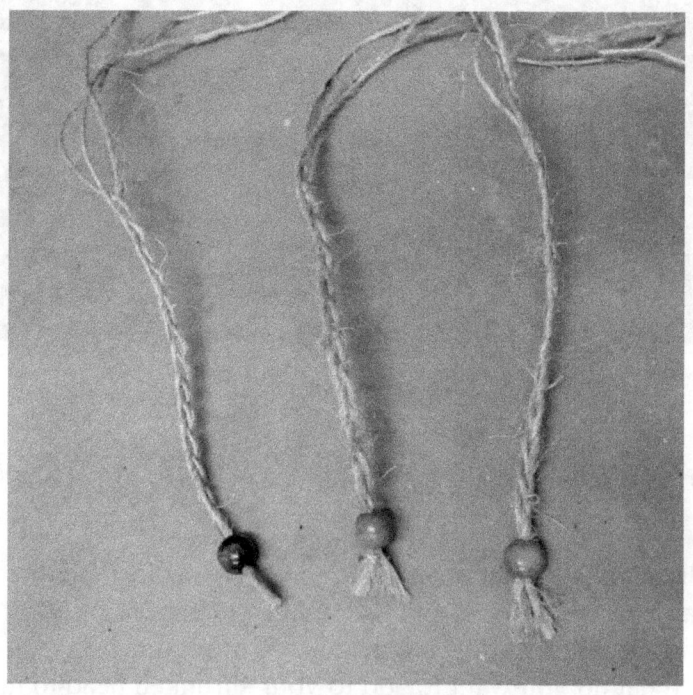

DIAGRAM 81

Shrunken Heads

I am going to start by sewing this guy's mouth shut. I have some twine here, but what is the best method of inserting the twine into the latex skin? I have a couple options I will share with you.

The first option is a modified hair punch style needle. All I did was replace the sewing machine needle with a hand-stitching needle that would typically be used to sew woven fabrics. It's a size 14 needle. I thread this needle the same way I did the sewing machine needle. I opened and sharpened the eye, then put the needle itself into a wooden dowel. The larger eye on this needle allows me to capture a thicker strand of material, like twine rather than hair.

The size 14 needle I used is really common and comes in a regular package of assorted hand-stitching needles you could find at almost any fabric store, big box store, or perhaps your grandma's sewing basket.

The other option I have, which might still be available to you, is a leather needle. It works well, but I did have to sharpen the tip to get it to puncture the latex. You can find these at most craft stores or specialty leather suppliers. It's pretty inexpensive. I have dozens that came with a lot I purchased at a local auction house.

With either of these tools you should easily be able to punch the twine into the lips of your shrunken head.

This is the stylistic sewn lips I came up with after looking at a number of references. You can do a simple cross stitch if you like. It doesn't have to be this over the top. The simple cross stitch will have a huge impact.

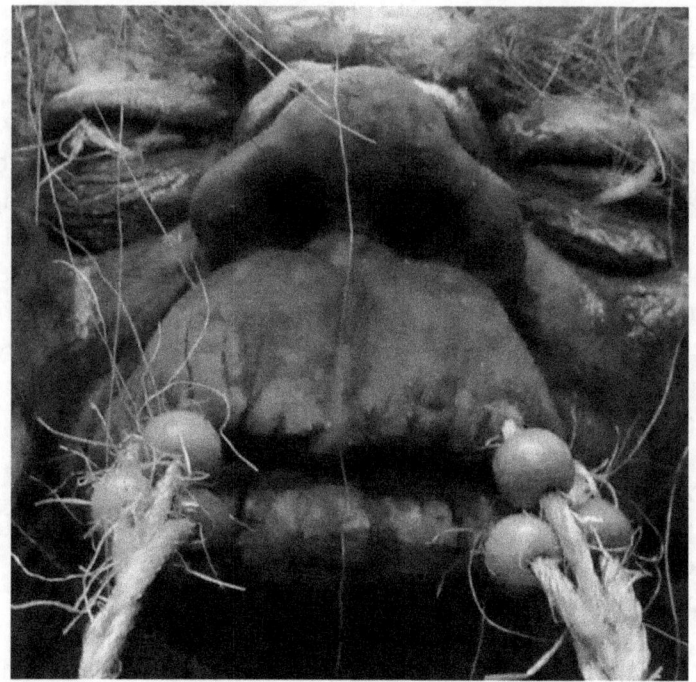

DIAGRAM 82

I am going to use the same method to sew the eyes next, but I will also expand the twine punching to the earlobes. I will punch the twine into the earlobe and run some wooden beads up the twine. I can use superglue or a simple knot to lock the beads in place. Now my shrunken head has earrings. And I used some beads that have been in the way for five or six months.

I was going to add a bone through the nose, but felt it might be a bit cliché. It's not like he is going to complain. I sewed him up good! The bone just didn't seem to fit the esthetic I am going for. Sometimes less is more.

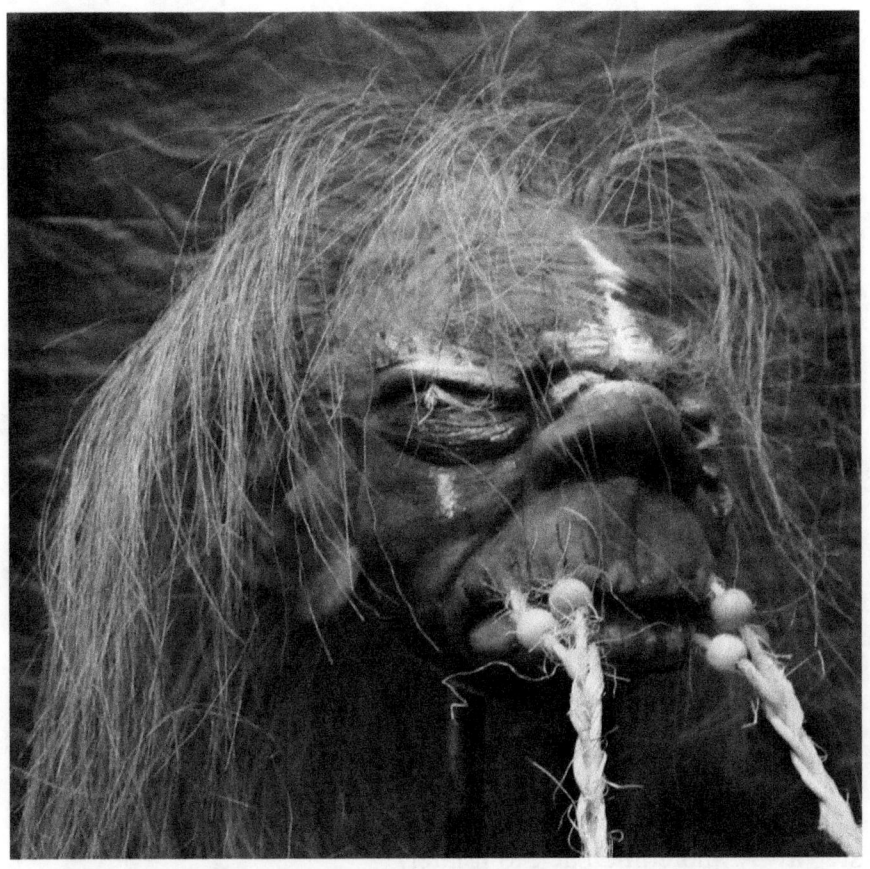

WORKSHOP SUMMARY

Let's do a quick review of what we learned in this book. From
making wooden and metal sculpting tools, to building your own
armature, you have learned that as a new artist you don't need to
purchase expensive tools to create amazing pieces of work.
Buying another artist's overpriced, low-quality tools isn't going
to make you a better artist, just a poorer one. Making your own
tools can be satisfying part of the process and it saves you money

while making use of scrap materials that would otherwise end up in a landfill.

You've learned important steps to sculpting—blocking, rough detail, and fine detailing. These steps will slow you down and allow you to focus. It isn't a race. These steps will also prevent you from repeating your efforts and from prematurely creating detail that might later be destroyed. Follow these steps each time you sculpt and you will do fine.

We discussed sealing your sculpture and the sometimes-terrifying prospect of molding it. My method isn't the only way to build a successful mold for your sculpture, but it's a tried and true process that has served me well for two decades. That said, I encourage you to watch other artists, learn from other tutorials. There is always a better way to do things. Take what you can from each method you learn and build on it. Until then, you have my method and a helpful checklist at the end of the book to guide you.

You learned how to demold a sculpture. Just remember to be patient and methodical about the process. If you are frustrated during a demold because something isn't separating properly, step away and come back to it later.

We also talked about mold straps and prepping a mold for casting. We talked about the casting process itself and how to demold a latex pull. This is probably the easiest part of the entire process. It's certainly not the most glamorous. There is nothing better than seeing that new shrunken head pop out of a mold--a clean pull with infinite possibilities.

I talked about the cleaning and seaming process and how you can correct any mishaps that may occur. From horrid air bubble attacks to flashing mishaps, you now know how to deal with just about anything a bad casting day can throw at you. Don't forget to visit that YouTube video on seaming. It's an older video, but the information still applies.

You learned that you don't need an airbrush to creature a professional paint job on your projects. Washes can be the name of the game. And who knew you could get a couple more uses out of those old sponges and upholstery foam? Oh, and good news for your kids. Finger painting can be a life skill.

Finally, you learned that painting isn't always enough to bring a mask to life. Sometimes it takes twine, intense hair punching, and maybe some wooden beads to finish it off.

I hope you have garnered a greater appreciation for other artists' work. When you see, an artist selling his/her wares, you should have a better understanding of the work that went into creating the pieces and why they are asking the price they are. You've just experienced what it takes to create just one shrunken head. How much would you sell yours for?

Mostly, I hope you gained the confidence to do this on your own—to take what I have taught you and put it to use. The biggest fear most people face coming into a project like this is the unknown. That's no longer the case for you. You know where to begin. You will become a better sculptor with time and practice. You know how to make this an affordable endeavor. And you now know what to do if you screw up.

So, have some fun and get to work.

MOLD MAKING CHECKLIST

(Feel free to add notes you feel are important for you to remember.)

Do you have all your molding materials on hand ready?
___10-25 lbs of UltraCal 30 Plaster
___A Yard of burlap cut into 3"x3" squares
___Petroleum jelly (release agent)
___A couple chip brushes
___A disposable cup for water
___Mixing sticks
___Dust mask or respirator
___Latex gloves
___Black marker
___2x4 scraps
___WED Clay (for the mold process)
___Mixing bowl
___Clear Matte Spray Paint

Have you sealed your sculpture with matte spray paint?

Building the Caseline
___Drawing a dotted dividing line with marker
___Pillow of clay covered with a sheet of plastic
___Gently lay sculpture back. Head resting face up and on the clay pillow.
___2x4 in place and secured with hot glued
___Use clay to build up to your dotted line-- DON'T TOUCH SCULPTURE
___Smooth the clay caseline
___Now the clay caseline should seamlessly meet the sculpture
___Retaining wall
___Make registration marks and place them against the retaining wall
___Seal the clay with clear matte spray.

Inspect areas for undercut hazards.
___Neck

___Ears
___Ear trench

Plaster Layer 1: The First Splash Coat
___Work out air bubbles
___Clean your brush. DON'T LEAVE IN WATER

Plaster Layer 2: The Second Splash Coat
___Work out air bubbles
___Clean your brush. DON'T LEAVE IN WATER

Plaster Layer 3: The Insurance Layer
___Lay burlap down on caseline first
___Overlap burlap
___Work from caseline up to the face of the sculpture.
___Work out air bubbles.
___Smooth surface with a brush
___ Clean your brush. DON'T LEAVE IN WATER

Plaster Layer 4: The Protective Layer
___Thicker mix. Playdough
___Watch air bubbles.
___Use brush to smooth surface
___ Clean your brush. DON'T LEAVE IN WATER

Name and Date on Side One

Prepping for Side Two
___Set sculpture upright
___Gently remove 2x4s (break hot-glue bond with rubbing alcohol)
___Remove the clay build-up
___Remove clay wall
___Set sculpture face down on work surface
___2x4s or clay to stabilize any wobbling
___Build side 2's retaining wall
___Cut and add pry marks and place them against the retaining wall.
___Petroleum Jelly coat on all plaster surfaces. CASELINE NOT THE SCULPTURE

Repeat above steps from PLASTER LAYER 1

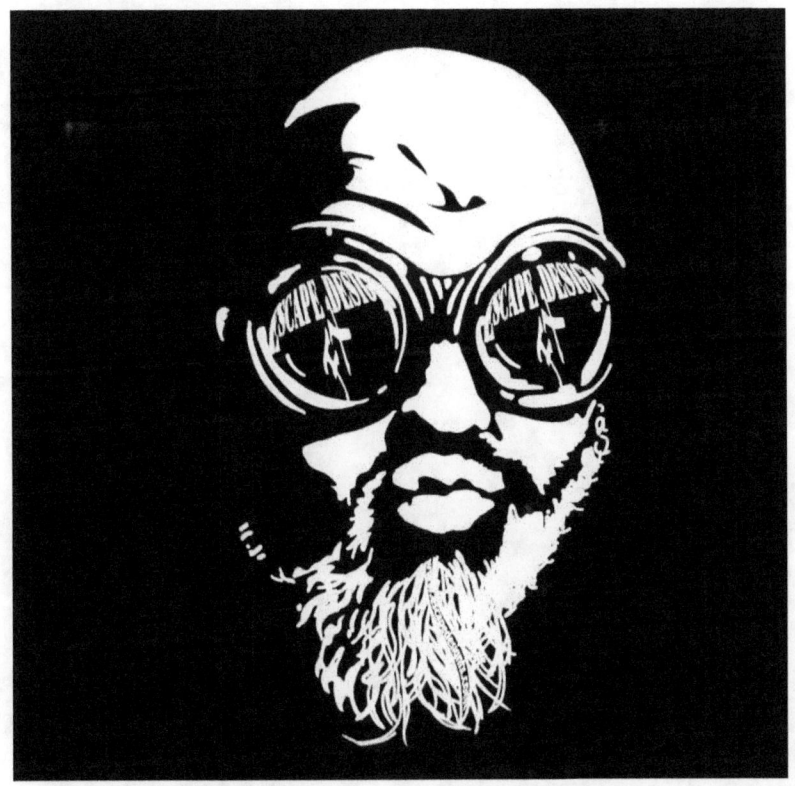

Additional Information

You can find out more about Russ Adams's work at the following URLs;
Author Page (including appearances): www.russadams.me
Contact info@russadams.com
Professional Page: www.escapedesignfx.com
Contact admin@escapedesignfx.com

Follow this author on social media
Facebook www.facebook.com/escape.design,
INSTAGRAM @AdamsRuss,
TWITTER @EscapeDesign,
YouTube EscapeDesignFX

More Workshops to Come

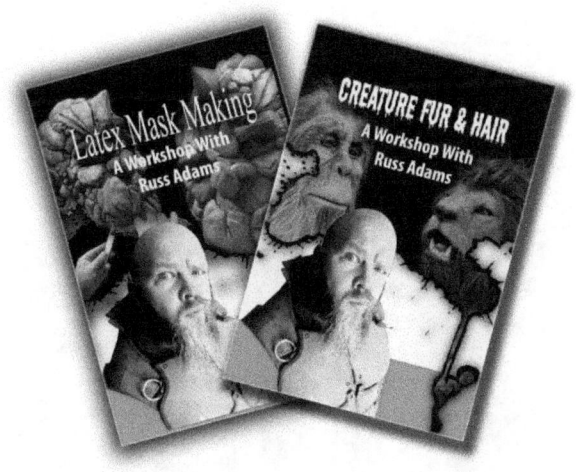

Russ Adams

PROJECT NOTES

PROJECT NOTES